YoungWriters 2005 CREATIVE WRITING
COMPETITION FOR SECONDARY SCHOOLS

T·A·L·E·S·

From Across The World
Edited by Lynsey Hawkins

Disclaimer

Young Writers has maintained every effort
to publish stories that will not cause offence.

Any stories, events or activities relating to individuals
should be read as fictional pieces and not construed
as real-life character portrayal.

Young**Writers**
First published in Great Britain in 2005 by:
Young Writers
Remus House
Coltsfoot Drive
Peterborough
PE2 9JX
Telephone: 01733 890066
Website: www.youngwriters.co.uk

SB ISBN 1 84602 299 1

Foreword

Young Writers was established in 1991 and has been passionately devoted to the promotion of reading and writing in children and young adults ever since. The quest continues today. *Young Writers* remains as committed to engendering the fostering of burgeoning poetic and literary talent as ever.

This year, *Young Writers* are happy to present a dynamic and entertaining new selection of the best creative writing from a talented and diverse cross section of some of the most accomplished secondary school writers around. Entrants were presented with four inspirational and challenging themes.

'Myths And Legends' gave pupils the opportunity to adapt long-established tales from mythology (whether Greek, Roman, Arthurian or more conventional eg The Loch Ness monster) to their own style.

'A Day In The Life Of ...' offered pupils the chance to depict twenty-four hours in the lives of literally anyone they could imagine. A hugely imaginative wealth of entries were received encompassing days in the lives of everyone from the top media celebrities to historical figures like Henry VIII or a typical soldier from the First World War.

Finally 'Short Stories', in contrast, offered no limit other than the author's own imagination while 'Hold The Front Page' provided the ideal opportunity to challenge the entrants' journalistic skills, asking them to provide a newspaper or magazine article on any subject of their choice.

T.A.L.E.S. From Across The World is ultimately a collection we feel sure you will love, featuring as it does the work of the best young authors writing today.

Contents

European School of Luxembourg, Luxembourg

Tom Clarke (12)   69
Sarah Graham (12)   70
Emily Simpson (12)   71

Falcon School Cyprus

Halil Halil (16)   72
Natasha Holmes (14)   74
Daria Kolmogorova (12)   75
Noeleen Advani (13)   76
Tara Tate (15)   77
Nicholas Papaxanthos (14)   78
Olympia Severis (14)   79
Sama Meibar (14)   80
Apoorv Bhargava (15)   82
Romy Wakil (16)   83
Gary-Thomas Aspell (16)   84
Anurag Rekhal (12)   85

Institut Montana, Switzerland

Edgar Haener (15)   86
Sabrina Bleuler (17)   88
Olexander Karpenko (17)   89
Marline Kipper (17)   90
Krystyna Liakh (17)   91
Westley Tsou (16)   92
Wandile Mzikababa Mngomezulu (18)   93

Ivy Thomas Memorial School, Uruguay

Sofía Posada (13)   94
Agustina Cordone (13)   95
Juan Pablo Rossolino (14)   96
Juan José De Feo (14)   97
Florenciq Gimene (14)   98

Morna International College, Ibiza

Kirsty Keatch (13)   99
Jack Walker (11)   100
Sophie Lonsdale Ross (13)   101
Dara Dorsman (12)   102

St Brendan's College, Buenos Aires

St Constantine's International School, Tanzania

St Joseph's School, Abu Dhabi

Villa Devoto School, Buenos Aires

The Creative Writing

Brightening Sky

A breeze whispered through the long grass, passing over the still forms of the dead, brushing dew from their cold skin. The grass was wet, glimmering eerily in the pale rose wash of pre-dawn light.

The air rushed up over the top of a single knoll, swirling about the still form which lay upon it.

He lay as though asleep, unmoving, one leg bent at the knee, the ankle nestled against the back of his other, straight leg. His left arm lay straight out to the side, palm up, his fingers slightly curled, limp. The right arm was bent, hand level with head. His head itself was tilted back and slightly towards the east, lips parted, as though with his dying breath he had sought the sun.

The lines of his countenance were soft, gentle yet strong. The sun was rising now, casting shadows across his face and bathing him in golden light, glinting off the elegant chain about his neck, shining on his wet hair, swept back from his face by the night's rain.

The light caught the wetness of his soaked clothes, gleaming off his chest and corded arms. Sword cuts were visible on his bare skin, straight and shallow slices created by swift blades of dancing steel and a bruise marred his right cheek, tendrils of night creeping up to his eye and across to his nose. There was a dark stain on his sleeveless shirt, a tiny hole in the fabric over his heart.

The garments clung to him and red had painted itself upon his neck and shoulder, a trickle of it curving round his chin from the corner of his mouth, to meet with more blood dabbled in the hollow of his exposed collarbone.

He looked peaceful, tranquil. His handsome face was still, his once bright eyes closed. The breeze rushed across his soft skin, stroking his face and lifting flower petals into the cool air about him.

The silence of the dawn was unbroken, as the sunlight pushed back the shadows, sweeping across the grasslands in one massive wave.

The grass about Tamako stirred briefly in a sudden gust of air and then all was silent once more, the great stone giants known as mountains gazing out over the world.

Liz Stevenson (14)
Aiglon College, Switzerland

Major Lesson For A Minor

The streets of New York … what a terrifying place. Just when you think life is sweet, faster than you can say bagel, hell can break loose.

Eleanor was a happy child of three, ignorant of the dangers lurking everywhere on Broadway. Stubborn, she wanted her own way, often running away from Grandma or her parents. Dad decided to break the habit.

One evening, when Eleanor was hopping ahead of them, they hid behind a mailbox, peering from the sides at the child.

Dusk played hide-and-seek with the tall towers. Rush hour commotion made peace with the roads. Cars honked, the underground buzzed beneath everyone's feet.

In a New York minute, Eleanor swirled around. She froze instantly. 'Mommy, where are you?' Not seeing them anywhere, she panicked, white bleaching the cheeks. Eleanor didn't like the empty feeling. Her world had just changed.

Strangers casually strolling seemed like marching soldiers, boot size 48, crushing her flat as a pancake. Trees across in Central Park swayed wildly in the breeze, became monsters, howled at her, ready to reach out and grab her.

Eleanor fell to the ground, two rivers of despair poured uncontrollably down her cheeks. Reassuringly, her parents popped out like Christmas presents running towards her, arms spread wide. Father looked at the whole drama. Eleanor kept on crying in relief, but Father was content. He had just taught his daughter a very important lesson.

Andrea Antoniou (13)
American Academy, Larnaca

A Small Adventure In a Big House

'Jack, what shall we do? I'm bored watching this dull movie.'

But Jack never answered back as his watery-blue eyes were fixed on the television. Suddenly, the doorbell of their mansion rang.

'Open the door John,' said Jack, switching off the TV.

John looked very suspicious indeed but finally he opened it and unexpectedly a rather stout man, with a huge scarlet nose and a cigar in his mouth, appeared in front of them. The children were petrified as the man said with a hoarse voice, 'Your father said to me to take you to your aunt's house but he didn't tell me the reason.'

The two clever boys understood that the man was lying because they didn't have any aunts. So John, pretending that he was going to the toilet, sent a message to his father's phone explaining what had happened during his absence.

'Why don't you sit here and take a rest?' asked John cunningly, after doing his job.

The weird man shot a glance at the enormous living room and then sat on a sofa. Suddenly, with a loud bang the front door swung open and their skinny father appeared, making his way towards them as fast as a rocket. 'Who is this man?' Father asked, hastily looking at the chubby guy. Without saying a word, the man dashed out of the house and vanished in the darkness.

'Immediately go to sleep,' said their caring father as he telephoned the police.

The excited children headed towards their bedrooms thinking about their distasteful day.

What a surprising time they had had.

Sipan Oknaian (13)
American Academy, Larnaca

How The Tiger Got His Stripes

Once upon a time there lived a huge tiger who was very greedy. His motto was - 'Always take the easy route'. Well that is exactly what he did; instead of hunting he bullied others into giving their food to him.

One day the tiger was extremely greedy so the monkeys gathered everyone in the jungle in order to stop the tiger. Unfortunately everyone was terrified of the tiger, thus nobody thought of revenge on him. A beaver happened to overhear the meeting. He thought, *what cowardly folk they are! Well I have to be brave; after all who knows, the tiger might just come prowling here!*

No sooner had he thought of that when indeed the tiger came. He looked like an enormous orange-white flame. 'Hand over your fish,' he snarled, 'or I shall eat you up in one big bite!'

The beaver immediately forgot his bravery and leapt into a lake. The tiger, full of fury, followed him. This proved to be a bad idea because the tiger got tangled in some weeds in the lake. He managed to clamber out and cursing the beaver, the tiger slouched away but his troubles weren't finished. No matter what he did he couldn't get rid of the weeds that stuck to his back. He pleaded the animals to help him but they wanted to get revenge so they somehow set fire to the poor tiger.

The tiger howled in pain, dashed to the lake and jumped in. Having relieved the pain, the tiger scrambled out of the lake and looked at his reflection. He had black stripes where the weeds burnt away so that's how he got his stripes and his temper.

Anastasia Shterenberg (13)
American Academy, Larnaca

Embraced By Death

Standing on the periphery of the cliff, Angeline resembled an angel. The playful spring breeze lifted her waist-long, golden hair and threw it across her face - the face that had once been so beautiful. Now, it was gaunt and as white as lilies. The wide, aquamarine eyes were red-rimmed and the thick, dark lashes clung together from the recently shed tears.

Cars hurried along the highway some ten metres away, waves broke far below and the minute lights of the city glimmered on the horizon, it was an ordinary night for everyone but her. For this night was her last one.

No longer able to contain herself, Angeline howled with rage and loneliness. She screamed like a wounded animal, until her throat was raw and throbbing. Even then, the emptiness that was inside her refused to leave.

Breathing heavily, Angeline stumbled even closer to the edge. After the agony of the past year, her yearning for death, for all the torment to be over, was as maddening and overwhelming as the desire of a drug addict for just one dose. It cruised through her blood, it made her heart beat thrice as fast, it was in every cell of her broken being.

Throwing a last look at the world around her, Angeline hurled herself off the cliff. She plummeted towards the serrated rocks beneath, the fabric of her chemise billowing behind her like wings, and a small smile played on her lips.

Moments later, death finally embraced her.

Yana Korotaeva (16)
American Academy, Larnaca

Hide-And-Seek

'Ninety … ninety-five … one hundred. I am coming and I will find you wherever you are!' As Peter opened his eyes, he found himself alone in the rough road of his neighbourhood. The sky was filled with a solid screen of black cloud. The full moon was playing hide-and-seek with the clouds.

He looked behind the bushes, on trees but he found no sign of his friends. He searched the houses of the neighbourhood one by one, looking for clues as to the whereabouts of his friends. He caught sight of the last house down the street. Nobody lived in that house. He thought that his friends were hiding in there.

The front of the deserted house was very sinister. It had tall brick gateposts half open and turrets along the roof. Big drops of rain were now beginning to splatter on him. He climbed into the house through an opened window to shelter from the rain.

Going up the circular staircase he noticed a portrait of a young girl. Suddenly he heard giggles. He turned around. He faced a girl, the girl on the portrait. She was short and skinny with a bony face and a sallow complexion. She was staring at him with her deep-set, black eyes. Peter could hear the blood booming in his ears. He stepped backwards and fell down the stairs.

Absolute darkness. Blood.

'Ninety … ninety-five … one hundred. I am coming and I will find you wherever you are!'

Nicolas Kourti (13)
American Academy, Larnaca

A Pianist's First Achievement

I opened my eyes. I felt like I'd forgotten where I was, who I was and what was happening to me. I didn't know I had butterflies in my stomach and why I had been awaken so early in the morning, so I just snuggled back into my bed.

Tick-tock, tick-tock went the clock. I sat bolt upright. The butterflies were turning into elephants now. The competition. It was today. I jumped up, sending a box of tissues flying and landing on top of my cat. She let out a screeching *miaow,* which sent me flying out of the room in panic.

Now it was everywhere. It spread like a cobweb to every corner of my body. At last, I got dressed, having ripped two pairs of tights in hysterics and having eaten five chocolates to calm down.

I was twelfth on the list. I wanted to get it over and done with, but I, by then, was so nervous that my hands were slippery, had to stand in the hall for another twenty minutes.

Trying to prevent the red paint flowing into my cheeks, I walked on stage, trying to look confident. It worked … I had done it. My first competition, my first prize.

Liana Akimova (13)
American Academy, Larnaca

A Tale To Tell

Do you believe in fairies, dragons, unicorns, imps and other magical creatures? Do they really exist or are they only simply fantasy?

My name is Richard and I really believe in this magical world. When I was a kid something very special but rare occurred to me; for one little moment I entered a special world full of fantasy and magic, with strange but extraordinary creatures. Maybe you would not believe me, but the tale that I am about to tell you is not craziness, it's real.

When I was a little boy I lived with my family, my mom and my dad. We lived in the forest in a little house that to me was the biggest and the most awesome house that had ever existed in my life. I remember that I was playing in the forest. I was climbing a tree, trying to reach the top, when I fell to the ground, losing my senses. After a few moments I woke up. My legs hurt a lot, however. I knew I must not return to my house because my mom would never let me play again in the trees.

I decided to sit on the ground, when a luminous and sparkling light appeared I front of my nose. The light flew in a very simultaneous way, so I curiously followed the light. It moved like the wind, very fast, until suddenly it stopped in a place that I could not recognise. It was a very rare and different place; it was a magical world.

The place, as I could remember, was full of tiny houses with chimneys, with many shafts. The most incredible thing was that it was full of magical creatures. Many sympathetic imps started to appear from behind the trees, many little people were walking in the little village, unicorns were playing and fairies were flying in the air. I was really amazed; I could not believe that a world of fantasy could exist. I rubbed my eyes once then twice, trying to wake up from this dream, but it was impossible. All the magical creatures around me were real, they were there.

I stood up there, looking at lighthouses that were all over the little village, until two kids. a girl and a boy came to me. These kids were the same age as I was; the only difference was that they were dressed like fairies. I remember they had large ears, their faces were painted with different colours and their shoes were like a kind of slipper.

The girl was dressed with a sparkling dress with white mesh and she had flowers in her hair. The boy had a green skirt and a green shirt also. I remember when they invited me to play with them. We rode on unicorns, played with them and climbed different trees. It was incredible. After we finished playing, the two kids gave me a little object with the shape of a unicorn and said bye to me.

Suddenly everything began to disappear. I remember I found myself alone in that place; my only company was the little object. Right now, I still have the little unicorn object, however, only I can see it. When I show any person the object, they consider me a crazy person because they can't see anything. Nevertheless, I know that a magical and extraordinary world full of fantasy lives in our world, in a very unusual and secret place.

Nisme Castro Abdel Krim (14)
American Academy, Larnaca

Imagine What Life Could Be?

I think of life as a dream. When you go to bed you return to your real life. When you wake up is when in your real life you go to bed. In your real life you may be a butterfly you might even be a cat or a dog. But what if life were actually a dream? Maybe one day you'll wake up and return to your real life. As you return it would be like any other day where you'd eventually forget your dream and continue living your life. Then you'll return to your dream life when you go to sleep in your real life.

This is all very confusing but as you think about it, it makes sense. When you return to your dream life you think your real life was just a dream that you had last night. When you return to your real life the next day, all your friends, teacher, parents, pets from your dream life are gone. They are just faded memories now. Once you return to your dream life all your memories return and the memories that were from your real life fade away. This goes on and on as long as you can imagine, it never stops.

In your real life humans might not exist they may be like aliens in your dream life. All of the inventions that were in your dream lives may now be like UFOs in the dream life. Humans may be a distant dream that only some people believe in. Life can be weird and confusing we never know what is going to happen next. That is why I think dreams are so short but seem like so long. Maybe when we wake up one day we will return to our real life and look at the time and realise it was all a dream. Then we look at the time and see that we were only asleep for five minutes.

You could be an alien planning to invade the Earth and you were dreaming of how it would feel to be a human. You might be living on a planet that in your dream life no one knows about. You could be anything just by using your imagination and you an be anything. With your imagination you can do anything.

Julie Butler (12)
Anglican International School, Jerusalem

Ghost Story

Hi, my name is Lura. I was born in Texas and this is my story.

My parents were ghosts, I was a ghost, all my family were ghosts. To be a ghost you have to die. I went to the black church when I was 95. I died there. Then I was born again as a ghost. I was chosen to be a ghost. The ghost king in Heaven said, 'You will be a ghost, you will have another life, since you have been good in life. You have helped aliens in space by giving money to Neptune …'

'Why thank you,' I said.

Being a ghost isn't that easy. You have to take a potion every night because that way you don't turn invisible. Once a demon wanted to capture me. I ran down a hall because I was so scared. He captured me in a bottle, I was 12. I had no idea what was happening. He killed me. When I opened my eyes, I was in Hell.

Snails! I knew it! I thought to myself. Now I am not a ghost, I am a demon … devil.

Be careful about how you die!

Cristina Barba (11)
Anglican International School, Jerusalem

The Hallowe'en Party

(Dedicated to Mr Toltz)

Princess Cristina opened the envelope. She found an invitation from Mayor Tintin of Tinyville, inviting her to a dress-up party! *Oh, how splendid!* thought Princess Cristina.

Since October 31st was approaching -'A Hallowe'en party!' she said and decided she would dress as Purple Planet's purple striped tiger. She searched around the house for materials and found all the right stuff. First, an old, mouldy shag rug (that was rolled up in the garage) became her furry orange coat with purple stripes across the back. Then, Princess Cristina decided her face looked too dull. She grabbed a black marker and drew whiskers - much better. 'Now all I need is shoes. I think my brother used to wear a pair of yellow All Stars … yellow is good enough!'

After going through her brother's mess-of-a-closet and locating his beat up yellow All Stars, Princess Cristina gathered up all the parts of her costume. 'Perfect!' she said as she admired her creation. 'Now, to put it all on …'

When everything was in order, she set off for Tinyville (three galaxies away) and arrived at Mayor Tintin's miniature castle. She was absolutely horrified to find all the men in black suits and ties and all the women in white dresses with flowers in their hair. There was Mayor Tintin standing all the way at the front with a - no it couldn't be! - *Minister* waiting close by!

'A wedding!' uttered the princess. She looked down at her furry costume. 'A wedding!'

Leila Nashashibi (11)
Anglican International School, Jerusalem

An Unpleasant Business

As Mr Huxtable and his wife walked to the restaurant, a little dirty boy in ragged clothes started following them.

'Sir, Sir!' he called.

Mr Huxtable looked back and said, 'I don't have any change on me, so don't disturb me anymore.' He said this without even going through is pockets for Mr Huxtable did not believe in charity.

The little boy continued to cry, 'Sir, Sir!' but Mr Huxtable did not turn back. He just ignored him.

The Huxtables entered the prestigious restaurant and sat at a table by the window. They could hardly believe it when they saw the little dirty boy clinging to the window, staring at them. What an unpleasant business!

'He will go away eventually,' said Mrs Huxtable, and continued talking about trivial matters.

But Mr Huxtable could not ignore the eyes piercing through his flesh so easily. He felt really uncomfortable. Anyway, it would be very rude to enjoy an exquisite meal in front of a starving boy, wouldn't it?

The waiter had no problem in changing them to a table in the back. And after a superb meal accompanied by excellent wine, the Huxtables forgot all about the unpleasant business.

When the waiter brought the bill, Mr Huxtable noticed nervously that he did not have his wallet on him. Where had he left it? What a terrible shame! What a disgrace!

The waiter returned and said, 'Sir, a little boy outside told me to pass on a message to you. He said you dropped something on the street.'

'Where is that filthy boy now?' cried Mr Huxtable.

'I am afraid he has left. He did not want to disturb you anymore.'

Mariana Pedró (17)
Belgrano Day School, Buenos Aires

Greek Mythology Cronus And Rhea

Once, we heard about the Greek myth of the creation, the god 'Chaos' meaning 'Gaping void' was the founder of all things. Chaos begot Gaea which means 'Earth'; Tartarus, which is the bottomless depth of the deeper world; and Eros, the god of love. Eros drew divinities together so they might produce offspring. Chaos produced offspring Night, while Gaea bore Uranus (the god of Heaven) and after him, produced the mountains, seas and Titans (another group of gods). The youngest and most important was cronies. Uranus and Gaea who came to join the heavenly bodies and the earthical things also gave birth to the Cyclops; one-eyed giants who made thunderbolts.

Uranus never wanted any of his offspring to succeed him and take over his supreme position by forcing back into Gaea, the children she bore him.

But unfortunately, the youngest child, Cronus thwarted his father, cutting his genitals and tossing them into the seas where the bloody foam gave birth to Aphrodite, the goddess of sexual love.

After wounding his father and taking away his power, Cronus became the ruler of the whole universe. But Cronus in turn, feared that his own son would supplant him. When his betrothed sister and wife, Rhea gave birth to offspring - Hestia, Demeter, Hera, Hades and Poseidon - Cronus swallowed them. Only the youngest, Zeus escaped this fate, because Rhea tricked Cronus. She gave him a stone wrapped in swaddling clothes to swallow in place of the baby.

Mercy Bello (16)
Demonstration Secondary School, Nigeria

The Orphan Who First Discovered A Yam

A long time ago there was great famine, so terrible that a man would take his daughter and sell her for food, saving only his son to inherit his home. The famine brought with it many evils. With things in this state, little attention was paid to orphans; they were left to die of hunger. They wandered about in the woods, eating roots. Some ate what was poisonous and died.

One day a young orphan saw, growing in the forest, a yam. He dug it up, and said, 'I will try it. For what is death?' So he baked it and when it was ready he ate it and having eaten it he found that it was good and moreover, that he did not die. After that he went on digging up yams, baking and eating them always. Eventually one of the elders noticed him, and asked, 'How is it that though children who have both fathers and mothers are starved, and some have died of hunger, you on the contrary are growing fat, as though the famine has not touched you?' So the orphan told him all and so he had finished the old man asked him to come and show him so they went together into the wood. He showed him the yam and dug it up and gave it to him. The old man looked at it for a long time and then said, 'It is like one type of crop which we had in the former days and which also bore fruit under the ground.' He baked it and ate and they showed all inhabitants of the wood, and there was no more famine in their land.

Titilayo Alegbejo (16)
Demonstration Secondary School, Nigeria

A Day In The Life Of …

I began to feel the pains around my back and abdomen; at first it wasn't too bad but as time went on it became intense and the next thing I knew I went blank. I must have fainted for when I tried to open my eyes, it was difficult and I could only open them slightly before they were closed again. The ray of light that came into my eyes was just too bright and all I could see was white light, I could hear people talking all around me pleading and willing me to wake up. Again I tried to open my eyes but still I couldn't because the light was just too bright, just then I heard a voice say, 'She's coming round.' It was his voice, it sounded so close.

Then I heard another voice say, 'Switch off that light.'

As I opened my eyes, all I could see were people in white. Was I alive or was I dead? Then I saw his face with a reassuring smile, I tried to smile back but I was too weak and still in pain.

He turned to one of the men in white and said, 'It's her first.'

Suddenly I felt a sharp pain and I screamed, quickly the people in white rushed around me and I heard one of them say, 'The baby is coming,' and they willed me to push and I did with all my strength. In a twinkle of an eye all the pain was gone and all I could hear was the baby crying. Everyone congratulated me and smiled at me, but I did not hear them because all I wanted to do was sleep, but this time a restful sleep.

Faith Adigun (17)
Demonstration Secondary School, Nigeria

The Reward Of A Greedy Animal

The tortoise, the most cunning and greedy animal among other animals, had a day in his life he would never forget.

The tortoise and his wife, Yanbo, were invited to a dinner at the house of his wife's parents. They went to the dinner gorgeously dressed in very beautiful and expensive attire. They were a sight to behold as they walked hand in hand to the dinner. The dinner was done in a magnificent manner which showed that a lot of money was lavished on the preparation of the occasion. There were different varieties of dishes which were to be served with assorted drinks during the course of the dinner. The delicious aroma of the food pervaded the air and drifted towards the nostrils of the tortoise and, as usual, the greediness of the tortoise took hold of him. He left the dinner table and went straight to the kitchen where the food was kept, he removed his cap and put some food in it. For the fear of being caught he hurriedly put back the cap on and went back to the dinner table. There he started sweating with heavy beads of sweat falling and soaking him, he then stood up and said he was going. His wife was surprised but before she could say anything he had fainted. She screamed and people rushed towards them, they began to fan him and removed his clothes. Sometimes later his wife asked them to remove his cap and low and behold his hair had been burnt off, he was badly bald, it was a great embarrassment. One, which I am sure, he will never forget and would tell the story to his children, who will now tell the story to their children and so and so forth.

The tortoise learnt the great lesson that greediness is bad and he turned over a new leaf.

Tolu Owolabi (15)
Demonstration Secondary School, Nigeria

The Inestimable Princess

Once upon a time there lived a girl named Binta who resided in a very small village. She was so beautiful that everyone preferred calling her the 'princess', her beauty was like that of a rose flower, she was respected by all in the village. Her parents had died while she was a little girl. The time came for her to find a husband, all the handsome men in the village nearby came to marry her, those in faraway villages, and even the most handsome and richest men in all the villages came to marry her, but to no avail, she turned them all down for as she said that all the men were not handsome enough to be her husband.

There was a certain man who lived in a faraway village who wanted to marry the princess, the man was so ugly that he was too shy to meet the princess, he decided to go to a witch doctor to make him look very handsome and fit enough to marry the beautiful princess. The witch doctor succeeded in changing the man but gave the man only seven days to pay back the remaining sum of money. The witch doctor said that if the man did not pay back his money in seven days' time his face would change to that a baboon, which the man agreed to.

The princess was so happy to see the man and she agreed to marry him. After the marriage, the couple were to return to their destination. On their way home, there was a mighty river which they had to cross but they could not because there was no boat. The days were running out fast and it was on the fourth day, they both had to wait four days before they would be able to cross the river.

On the night of the seventh day the man felt that his head was heavy and knew that he had changed to a baboon as the witch doctor had earlier told him. He decided to run away before the princess could wake up.

When the princess woke up the next morning and could not find her husband she was worried and went searching for him. The princess later found out what had happened to her husband and that he would never come back to her. She wept and wept until her tears were flowing like a river, but yet there was no one to give her a helping hand and, from then on, she learnt a very tragic lesson, which she never forgot throughout her life.

Maobong Amos (15)
Demonstration Secondary School, Nigeria

A Day To Remember

Quincy the rat worked hard trying to gather up food because it was harvest time. As he worked, Clency the dog came and got all he worked for threatening to kill Quincy if he shouted. Out of fear, Quincy took to his heels appearing in his house in a twinkling of an eye.

Quincy cried asking God why he had created him so small and why he'd allowed the dog to exploit him anyhow.

Clency was not satisfied with his mischievous deeds and went further to murder Quincy's children. Quincy was so frustrated that he prayed asking God for divine intervention because all others had tried stopping Clency from his wicked acts, but he refused, saying he was their lord.

One day, Lion travelled from his continent to Quincy's town on research. On seeing how they were being tormented by Clency as always, he decided to tell Clency that there was one far greater than him.

Fortunately for Quincy, Lion was passing by. He asked Clency, 'What are you trying to do?'

Clency answered him with a hot slap. With great fury Lion lifted Clency from the ground and threw him like a football. Clency landed fifty centimetres away on the ground.

With great shame, Clency ran to the point of running faster than his legs. That ended the exploitation of Clency on Quincy. Quincy promised to respect Lion ever and always for that. It was a day for both Clency and Quincy to remember.

Martha O Egwa (17)
Demonstration Secondary School, Nigeria

Stairs!

When Gemma was little she fell down the stairs. Only we don't know how she got out of her room …

It was a sunny summer's day. I could see my dad cooking at the barbecue and my mum setting the table. I could hear Gemma crying because she wanted to get out and play. The food smelt delicious.

'Bek. Will you clear the table while I put Gemma to bed?' my mum asked me.

'Sure,' I replied.

I saw my mum closing the baby gates to make sure Gemma stayed upstairs.

We watched a video and after I decided to go to bed.

'Night,' I shouted from the hallway.

'Night!' my mum and dad shouted back.

When it was ten Gemma started to cry for a bottle, which was weird because she normally slept through the night. My mum came up and gave her a bottle and when she went back down I heard the gate click. It was locked.

At ten thirty my mum and dad went to bed. I heard them locking the gate, brushing their teeth and then going to sleep …

'Argh! Gemma's fallen,' my mum shrieked.

My dad grabbed the phone and stabbed the number in.

'Hello, I need an ambulance at 29 Wardrop Road,' my dad raced to say.

My sister is fine now, she only had a broken leg. She was unconscious for about half an hour. We don't know who opened the gate or Gemma's cot though …

Rebecca Clare (12)
Derby School, Germany

The Red Letter

A couple of weeks ago something happened. I still don't know how it happened. Was it my friends or had some strange power taken over?

That question still lies unanswered like something forgotten in an old dusty attic. It happened at Derby School, I still go there. It just seemed a normal day … but it wasn't!

When I got to school all my friends were there, I still blame them a little for what happened. The day had gone quickly, it was lunchtime already. I had to go to Prince Rupert School that night, 'How fun that's going to be!' we all laughed. Maybe if I hadn't told them, this wouldn't have happened. 'Can we play 40-40 in?' I asked

I *so* regret playing it now!

I went to hide and there it was, in the root of the old oak tree. It said my name on it, so bit by bit I opened it.

To my horror it said *'Don't go to PRS'* in scarlet letters. I just thought it was a joke at first but now I don't know.

When I got home I had the note tightly in my hand. I calmed myself down. We were on our way to Prince Rupert School and I felt sick so I nodded off. A loud bang woke me up. My legs were stuck under the seat …

We never got to PRS, but worst than that I'll never be able to play 40-40 again.

Sophie Gladstone-Sutcliffe (12)
Derby School, Germany

The Missing

It was your average Saturday morning. I was playing outside with Jana and Paige when suddenly we came across this house. I knew who lived there, it was Annabelle. My friends told me to go and call for her, but as I opened the gate the house vanished. I panicked so I called the police.

You wouldn't have thought that this would have happened. It was just a hot Saturday on 1st May. The month of May will never be the same again.

The police were helpful. They even called in a paranormal investigator. She shouted out, 'Where are you Annabelle? If you are here come forward and speak to me!'

There was no reply.

The investigator tried a new theory, travelling through time. With this theory you can have only two people. So Sarah went. At first she didn't want to go, but after she'd thought about it, she went. The investigator and Sarah huddled together and set off.

To start off with, they found nothing. Then they saw something amazing, it was a time machine right where the house was. They couldn't believe it.

They travelled back and told everyone what they'd seen.

'The house was actually built on a time machine,' shouted Sarah.

Then from out of nowhere a light flickered from a hole in the ground where the house was built. We all rushed over to see what had happened.

I turned round to see if anyone was behind me. I saw a little girl playing with a doll house. The house looked like the missing house. I went to see. I looked inside the doll house. There was Annabelle …

Charlie-Jade Martin-Stuart (12)
Derby School, Germany

Doll's House

It's weird. I mean, how it happened was really weird. I can remember it like it was yesterday.

I want to abandon it, but I can't. When I try I stop and think of Jenny. I miss her smile, laugh, even her temper tantrums, I miss her. My family will never be the same again because we moved to that old, creepy mansion.

When I opened the heavy door a high-pitched squeak droned through the air. A thick layer of dust covered furniture and door handles. In my room there was a doll's house on a table. That night I kept hearing strange noises. The next morning my teddy was gone.

As I walked out of my room I saw my teddy in the doll's house, it was tiny, as if it were the doll's.

Dad was out and Mum was busy so she wouldn't listen. I ventured upstairs and found Jenny sat to perfection by the dolls' house.

She was transfixed with it. Jenny was gruesomely sucked into it. colours flashed viciously, sparks flew around, screams and laughs murmured everywhere. Everything stopped.

She was sat in the doll's house. I picked her up and clutched her to my chest. A tear poured down my cheek. I think she wanted to cry. She couldn't. She was just a doll. The other doll's face had totally changed, it was enigmatically smiling.

This happened three years ago. All I can do is ask myself, 'Is she alive?' And, 'Is she in *there?'*

Hannah Smith (12)
Derby School, Germany

Rags

Sitting on the cold floor, in torn rags, it's hard to believe that just about two weeks ago I had been sitting on a warm bed. Mum had been alive then.

No respect. No respect at all, after all I did for them. All that nurturing and I don't even get a thanks. Well, I'll show them! All of those children that never show gratitude towards a loving mother, especially those who run away from them to live on he streets. Ingratitude, that's what it is!

I miss Mum so much. I miss the way she would tuck me in at night and I miss the way she would lull me to sleep. She would be there when I woke up from a nightmare. Dad died when Noor was a baby, and when he was alive he was hardly ever home. I can't stand to think of losing Noor, she's all I have left.

Time to get up, and rub all the sores and bruises on my back. Then start begging. Best not wake Noor, my little sister; otherwise she'll start crying and whining. So I leave her sleeping on the rags in the shadow of two buildings. When I've got enough money, I'll buy some fresh bread and wake her for breakfast.

There's a cycle you see, first the parents take care of their defenceless babies, and then when the parents are old and weak, the once defenceless little babies take care of their parents. But you see, the children on the streets don't have any parents to take care of them, so I have decided I will help them. When I die, I'll have the satisfaction of having helped someone in my pathetic life.

If you've never killed someone you don't know how incredible it feels, it's kind of like an addiction. I have helped those miserable souls more than they could have ever realised, and if they came back to life I am sure they would thank me.

It was a cold night, the perfect time to do what I did, I was pretending to go out for a stroll. I was wearing typical old lady clothing, that you come across in the street, nothing too flashy, soft colours.

I went for a scrawny little girl sitting on rags, between two buildings. I put on an inquisitive face, and asked her if she had anywhere to go. Then in a sorry face, politely, if she'd like a night stay in a house with a roof over her head and a meal. The filthy rag followed me eagerly. When we got to my house I told her to get some clothes from the cupboard, while I got her some food. I got a knife and slipped in behind her.

Disposing of her was easy since she was so tiny. I put her in a bin bag with some trash and threw her out into one of those huge trash cans in the street. One less burden in the world!

It's not easy to get money by begging. First you look unfed and feeble to gain pity. Having a little child near you like Noor helps especially when you are only ten yourself. Then there are three types of people: the genuinely helpful type, the ones that pretend not to see or hear you, and the ones that have a look of disgust and hatred written on their faces. Usually the last type go through a lot of trouble to avoid you.

I spot a couple of the first type. I could use Noor's help now. I run back to wake her up, but she's not where I left her …

Anam Rahman (13)
Dubai College, Dubai

Consequences

(An Extract)

3, 2, 1 …

'Joe if you don't get your act together I swear that I will throw you on the streets and by golly you'll learn a few things out there my son!'

I could almost count the seconds until Dad would blow up. Confused? Join the club. Quite recently, about a month ago now, but who's counting? My mum disappeared. Meaning we have no idea what happened to her. All we know is that she's not with us … Now it's just me and Dad. I'm not saying that we were all one big rerun of The Brady Bunch when Mum was here, but I always knew that when I left the house the door would be unlocked when I got back, that I wouldn't have to climb through the garden fence hoping the back door was open, and when it wasn't, having to sleep on the garden deckchairs and wake up feeling half dead. Sounds horrible doesn't it? 'Child abuse'. What would you have done? Right now I bet you're sitting in a nice chair probably in a dry building where it's safe … warm … wondering what the hell I'm talking about. If you were here in person I would probably say you wouldn't want to know and walk off but you're not, so …

'Lizzy sounds a bit too babyish for my liking. I guess I'll just stick with Liz. Liz. Short and sharp. Straight to the point. Sounds innocent too doesn't it? Innocent. Uncorrupted by evil or wrongdoing; sinless. Interesting … Revenge. Even more fascinating. My husband was mobbed and killed outside his office building. Right there in the open. I was worried sick at home staring at the clock in the kitchen, sipping a cold cup of coffee. 'What ifs' were running through my head. Coppers. 'Your husband … I'm very sorry' … They started to explain how they'd found him under bags of rubbish. A backpack was still hanging on his shoulder. It was empty. His throat was slit several times and blood covered him and everything around him. A tag was round his neck.

'You don't care … so neither do us', it had read. The cops said that they've been trying to catch this mob of homeless for years and that was that. Well thanks for the help you lazy buggers!

My dad. The boss. The big man … You would think it's normal for the dad to be in charge, make important decisions and pay the bills, blah, blah, blah.

'It's not unusual for you dad to be slightly overprotective especially after the disappearance of your mum, Joe.'

Counselling. Didn't do me any good. They don't know anything …

My dad used to be in the army. Sergeant major. When Mum was with us you would think that he was a shy man destined for a desk job. Wrong. Underneath all that was his real hard core personality. Suddenly she goes and it decides to reappear. Blast from the past you could say. It's like living with the Hulk. Unpredictable …

Michelle Bushill (13)
Dubai College, Dubai

Stone Cold

(An Extract)

How have I ended up here? How have I ended up here in this good-for-nothing place? I thought it would be easier than this. After all hundreds of people do it every day - run away from home. I've finished all the food I brought with me and now I'm here on the street begging for money. But whatever happens, I'm not going back home.

Not back there I'm not. I wonder what everyone is doing at home right now ... Mum ... well she's probably drunk as usual ... probably got into a fight down at the pub again. But I know she doesn't care that I'm gone. She doesn't care about her 'Little Dougie'. 'Little Dougie' ... I remember when she used to call me that. Things were different back then. Dad was here for a start. Mum had a job, she didn't drink, she was a respectable woman. Things changed when Dad left though. He was a right git anyway. Mum became an alcoholic and got into all sorts of trouble at the pub and stuff. Then she'd hit me and Keira for no reason. I wonder what Keira's doing now. Her life wasn't exactly all rainbows and butterflies either. She was probably with Gary, her boyfriend. I never liked that guy. I knew something was up when she started getting bruised and wore bandages all the time. It was so obvious that Gary was abusing her, I don't know why she didn't just leave him.

Anyway, you can see that things were tight at home and I was the only one who could keep the family going ... but I was only 15. How can anyone expect a 15-year-old to keep a family together? So as you can see, I had no choice but to leave the place. I regret it sometimes. I just left the house with a few quid, an old tattered sleeping bag and some essentials, like my toothbrush. But I didn't think things through. I didn't realise the fact that I'd end up with no money at some point, the fact that I was too young to get a job.

So here I am, on the street outside some cheap cosmetic shop in Hastings. I've tried looking for a job. You know, the jobs where you clean tables at restaurants and stuff. I was looking for a job that could give me enough money to buy a decent meal. But no luck at all. One look at the state of me and they go off laughing, thinking that I'm some type of joke or something. And plus, it's Hastings, a quiet place, not many jobs available either. I'm thinking about leaving this place and going somewhere new and fresh, somewhere I can start again. Somewhere like London. All that is impossible though because I'm out of dosh.

I still remember that day … that day they told me to leave. What were they thinking? I was a qualified man. I could do much more than be just a prison officer. Prison officer. Honestly. I tried to do more, I really did. I had potential to do much more than sit and watch some depressed lowlifes behind bars. So I hung out with the 'real' police officers and tried to get the criminals, the druggies mostly. The way the people just sit on the streets begging for some money and then go away and spend it all on drugs, honestly, they are ruining the country, that's what they're doing.

So that's what I told the big guy down at the police station but they used that as an excuse to fire me … can you believe it?

'Stay away from them … you're a prison officer, Toby,' that's what they said to me. But I'll show them better. I'm going to clean up the streets of Hastings and make our country more respectable. Especially those kids. Family problems, that's what they say but really it's their lives taken over by drugs. So here I am, devising a plan to get rid of these bleeding druggies on the streets. It might be nasty but I'm not going to let that aspect let me down. I'm a clever man, I can think of something … anything to get rid of them. I look at myself in the mirror … 48 years old and still a handsome young bloke at heart. I look around my flat. Not too shabby but could do with a few touch ups. My plan is to lure them good-for-nothings here and take care of them the proper way …

Priyanka Patel (13)
Dubai College, Dubai

Addicted

(An Extract)

Your worst day would probably be my best. You probably take all the little things you have for granted; even having a bed is more than enough for me. Small, narrow, hard. Anything is better than a hard concrete floor, which I have to sleep on. I have been doing this for a month. I kept telling myself I wouldn't be able to survive and I would go back home but every day it seemed harder to go back. Now it's definitely been too long to even think about going home. But I haven't completely given up hope. My mother and I didn't end things very well, however, she might come back. I mean, I am her daughter.

I'll explain from the very beginning. I know what you people think. A girl on the streets. It must be her fault. Or in some of your cases you don't even notice us. I admit it's not all because of my family, the little I have, that I am on the streets. My mother, she had me when she was 16, the same age as me now. She didn't really treat me very well, but I shouldn't complain; anything is better than my 'life' now. I never knew my dad and it seems like I never will. That's why when my mother threw me out I didn't have anyone to go to.

Friends? Well school on its own had a lot to do with it. I used to be an A* student. No one would ever guess that now. I look like I've never had a shower in my life! My tangled hair, grey dirty face, shabby clothes. When you're on the streets none of the money you have, if you actually have any money, is used on clothes. It's all spent on food, cigarettes or drugs. But not me; I have stopped now.

As you might know, if you are a very good student (like I said I was), the only people who talk to you are bullies trying to get your answers and of course the teachers. I had no friends. Until one day I saw a large group of Year 11s. One year above me. I had never noticed them and I thought they might not know about me. So I decided to try my luck and went up to talk to them. One of the worst decisions of my life and I have made many bad decisions! I saw them all around the tallest of the girls. She was fairly pretty with long brown hair. She was holding a bag full of green stuff. You can see by this how innocent I was; I didn't know what drugs looked or smelt like. She surprisingly asked me if I wanted to try some. Obviously I said yes; I didn't want her to tell me to go away. She gave me the first batch for free and told me next time I'd have to pay for them.

That's how I became addicted, it only took one puff and it felt amazing. All my problems at home with my mum, the pressure of always having to do well, it all went away. After that I used to meet them every day after school. I started changing, wore my mum's make-up, her clothes. This made her get angry but I didn't care. I couldn't lose my so-called friends …

Minaal Khan (13)
Dubai College, Dubai

Amazing Animal

There it is lying in the fresh dried hay. Its eyes staring through the lands of Africa. The animal is getting attracted to food while it is lying there quietly. The antelope is keeping watch for its predator. Yes indeed it is the fast, talented *cheetah!* Day and night it relaxes while it is looking for food and stays in good form. The cheetah has very strong legs which makes it dig to the ground and run as fast as it possibly can. The cheetah grabs its prey by its long strong claws, digging into the skin of the antelope. The cheetah is already on its way home to feed its young ones. All at the same time, the young ones are feeding with their teeth through the juicy meat.

A couple of minutes pass and all that lies there are bones. The cheetah feels full and takes a nap. Under the wonderful trees in the plain field of dried hay, they lay underneath. Enjoying the small breeze flowing through their fur. As the day passes, the sunset comes to an end. When the night comes to a big exciting start, the cheetah enjoys spying and seeing if any other creatures are enjoying a night walk. With glowing eyes the cheetah can see very well in the night. It finds food for breakfast easily. The night passes very shortly and the cheetah wakes up by the sun shining into its eyes. The cheetah is a dangerous creature but a great animal.

Basil Schneeberger
Ecole Nouvelle de la Suisse Romande, Switzerland

A Day In The Life Of Jennifer Lopez

At 8am I'm waking up because I must be ready for a photo shoot for the *Girl* magazine. It's always the same: be the superstar during the shoot and then what?

I think they must be kind with us after the shoot not only to give us the money.

10.30am - I must be ready to do an interview for the *Salut*. They are not always kind with me. Sometimes they criticise me and then a week later they say very nice things about me.

They destroyed mine and Ben Affleck's relationship. I think they are jealous that two stars can have affection together. Immediately they invent things about the stars like a secret relationship and things like that. It really affects me.

13.30pm - I'm waiting for my best friend, Emma, to come and we will eat something at the pub next to my house. The problem is that when I arrive at the pub there are already four photographers. I like to be a star and to be popular, but now I have no privacy. I feel very badly towards my friends that are not stars because if they don't want to be in the photos then I can nearly never see them in a restaurant.

It's always the same things to do every day. It's not always easy to be a star. Trust me!

Alison Argi (12)
Ecole Nouvelle de la Suisse Romande, Switzerland

Anger Is The Key

'Stop it! Be quiet!' I screamed at him. But he continued. He kept telling me something that I didn't like hearing. *'Why don't you take on a role? What about being our dog for a day? Describe it! Or what about being … the lawnmower? Place yourself on the ground and imagine how it feels to go back and forth, chewing grass …'* Argh! What stupid and ridiculous ideas, especially in the middle of a relaxing Chinese meal.

The restaurant was calm, especially in the corner where we were placed. The restaurant was new, so I wasn't surprised that the waiters were extremely nice to us. Ten minutes after we ordered, the fantastic presentation of Chinese food arrived at our table.

From my calm posture I felt anger begin to bubble up inside me. It slowly took over, beginning from my feet and finally reaching my head. Heat was what I felt. I couldn't contain it anymore. I found myself standing up and shouting at him to stop! But he wouldn't listen. He just kept babbling! That made me even madder! How could I let out my frustration? More importantly, how could I stop him?

Then after all, those ideas were not so bad and his intentions were good. He is after all my father, so it all ended up with a big hug and an idea for this story. But what would I call it? And then it struck me: Fear! But for me it's not about fear, it's about anger …

August Roos (12)
Ecole Nouvelle de la Suisse Romande, Switzerland

Hold The Front Page

The new technology!

Technology has evolved so much over the years. They have now invented a new portable music player. The iPod! It's a system to listen to music without carrying CDs all over the place. They come in different sizes, colours and store many things such as music, pictures, games amongst other things.

Recording music is easy. Just pop a CD into the computer, click the important transfer button and the music will be transferred to your iPod in less than five seconds. iPod lets you listen to your music for up to 18 hours on a single battery charge.

The most used iPod is the 'iPod Mini' because of its size and weight. Select your 'iPod Mini' to match your outfit. Whether you prefer 'Pretty Pink' or 'Yer Blues', iPod Mini turns heads with every tune you play.

Technology at work for the modern girl (or boy)!

Nicole Britton (12)
Ecole Nouvelle de la Suisse Romande, Switzerland

Dead End

I can't describe properly the feeling I was going through that morning. I awoke on the rough, spiky bed that I had tried to make as comfortable as possible. I had made my decision and I was more positive about it than I had ever been about anything before. I was experiencing so many mixed emotions but I felt so wonderful.

My mind was whirling around so fast but I knew that I had made the right decision because I was confident about it. I felt happy and I had the tiniest feeling of excitement creeping up inside me that was making my stomach spin and my head thump harder and faster than ever. I should imagine that my stomach spinning and my heart thumping so furiously had something to do with nerves because I have to admit it now, that I was slightly nervous … okay, I was extremely nervous! What if none of it worked out the way I had planned? What if things became worse for me than they were already …?

Well, I went through with it anyway.

Time was getting on so I decided to stop sitting around doing nothing, wasting time and worrying about everything. This was it. I had made up my mind and I was going through with it. I couldn't go on living like this, this horrible, torturous and treacherous life. No, it was time to move on and leave it all behind. I was stuck and everything had gone too far … enough was enough.

I left my little home, if you could call it that, and walked on, not even glancing back. I knew exactly where I was going. It would take quite a while to get there but I didn't care. I was so full of energy that it was making me quite giddy. Well, I may as well have made the most of my last moments there by being happy, so I skipped along across the empty wilderness, humming one of the friendly songs we used to sing back there on the few days we weren't working.

To think that I had thought that everything would be better for me by running away from that place. I stopped. I had arrived and could just about see the cliff edge in the distance.

Standing as still as a statue, my body tensed, I gulped some fresh air as somehow I had forgotten to breathe. I closed my eyes, took a deep breath and thought through each stage of my life and what I was about to do. Still with my eyes closed, I took a heavy step forward, feeling all shaken up and stiff and scared. I took another step forward and another and another. Eventually, I started walking a bit faster. Suddenly I stopped and stood still. This didn't feel right, it wasn't meant to happen like this. Why was I so nervous? I was meant to be happy and excited about it.

I opened my eyes and looked around. I waited for a bit, almost as if I were actually waiting for someone (I knew I wasn't because there was no one else around).

I stopped waiting and took a deep breath and smiled to myself. I went straight for it, running and running, faster than I had ever run before. I felt as though my feet were lifting off the ground. The wind was blowing in my face and I felt a cold, relaxed and excited shiver thrill down my spine. This was more like it. I was confident and happy and everything felt free and smooth. I knew that this was the end of this life and the beginning of a new, wonderful life.

Still smiling and still running faster than ever, I jumped. And what a jump it was! I jumped as though I was carrying no weight at all. I didn't really have much weight, seeing as I had never had a decent meal in my life.

Oh I felt so free just flying in the air like that. No, I wasn't scared at all anymore. It was such an overwhelming feeling, falling. I didn't believe I was falling. I truly believed I was flying.

The sound of laughter came rushing out of my mouth and I was smiling now with so much joy. It was a refreshing feeling and I was filled with happiness, excitement and most of all, freedom! I never wanted this feeling to end, until … *bang!*

So here I am, dead, as you would call it.

Natasha Ward (14)
English International College, Málaga

A Day In The Life Of Eva Banning

Dear Diary,

Today was pretty average; nothing really happened, nothing at all. In fact, no one even talked to me, not that anyone ever does really. I'm not really surprised, I'm kinda used to it.

My lunch was quite fun. No one teased me, although I was sitting in the toilets alone, picking at my sandwich. No one sat with me, but I quite enjoyed having lunch peacefully. But my peace and tranquillity was destroyed as soon as Sasha and Gena entered the bathroom (as they do every lunchtime). As usually they fixed their hair and make-up and giggled about various things, like boys and other girls. I found it quite challenging not to smirk and laugh a lot, but then my name came up ... 'Eva is so weird and a drama queen, so selfish. I think it might be illegal to be that dorky.'

Now, I was quite used to this sort of stuff, but at that moment I snapped. My eyes welled up with tears and my heart broke. See I knew I was unpopular but maybe I'd had enough, that's right, I'd had enough. I was sick of people isolating me, alienating me, I mean, it can't be them, it's me, I'm abnormal.

It's 1am, I don't want to wake up tomorrow. My whole life and existence seems surreal, like a nightmare, but I'm awake. My life is an endless black cloud ... I have now cried myself to sleep.

I feel the sharp, cold steelness of the knife. I hope I never wake up.

Aimee Watkinson (14)
English International College, Málaga

A Day In The Life Of My Dog Harvey

6.30am   Hello, since no one's awake I'll introduce myself. My name's Harvey Mills. I'm five years old, but I act like a baby, in such a way that I'm scared of most things like the vacuum cleaner, the hair dryer and so on. I hate cats, like most clever dogs do. One of my best tricks is to sneak out of the gates when no one's looking but recently they all seem to have clicked on to my clever tricks. Like when I was two I used to climb up onto the roof, run across it and jump onto the neighbour's hedge and then run through their garden and out their gates, that was until they put a fence to stop me from jumping onto the roof from the balcony.

7am   No one's awake. Oh well, I'll hang on the door until they come and let me out. It's starting to smell in here. Maybe I should have hung on and not had an accident on the floor.

7.10am   Finally I'm outside having my breakfast. What a fuss Dad's making over the accident on the floor, all that heaving for nothing, it took them like two seconds to clean it up.

8.45am   Everyone's out the house. I'll have a quick nap before Mum gets home and takes us for a walk on the beach.

9.30am   This is the life, swimming in the sea and running on the beach.

10.30am   We've just got home and I'm outside having a rest, after being shouted at to get outside. So shoot me, I'm wet. How would they like it to have to sit outside? I want to have a sleep in my bed, but no, I'm wet.

1pm   Mum's gone shopping. It's time for me to have a bit of time to myself watching 'Neighbours' on the sofa, they would have a fit if they knew what I do when they're out.

10pm   That was a day of success. I got a lot done. See you in the morning, night.

Alex Mills (13)
English International College, Málaga

Stay Under The Covers

Hey, my name is Denny. My story starts two years ago in the darkness of my old house in my room. I hated it there, and I never could sleep. Every night I stayed under the covers.

I'm thirteen years old now and I live in dirty, skanky, but wicked London. Thankfully, I now live far away from the terrifying house, it was all the way in the middle of Wales. The reason we moved I will tell you now, so get ready for the fright of a lifetime.

It started when I first encountered 'the spirit'! And I kept on telling them and they never ever believed me, until they saw it themselves. They were scared stiff.

Every night from then on the ghostly figure came into my room and decided to pick on me. It came in and I could see it, and it pointed at me and walked closer and closer and closer. I wanted to scream but nothing came out, so I had to hide under the covers. I thought it would help and it did, cause he was gone when I looked. Then one night I couldn't move and he was coming nearer. He said to me, 'Quick, get out, I'm a nice spirit but the others aren't, they will hurt you, so get out of this house, and quick.'

So we stayed a little while longer but it carried on so we decided to move and here I am and this is my story.

Denny South (13)
English International College, Málaga

Touched With Fire

Where am I? Who are you? Who am I?

I'm Jamie 13 and I've been severely burnt in a fire. Those were the first questions that entered my head as I awoke inside the hospital. Then I felt the pain and looked down at my body. I could see the burnt swollen flesh, which has made me look unwanted.

Slowly the memories returned and I began to piece together what had happened. It started in the kitchen. Some boys came in with petrol and matches. I tried to stop them but they just threw me in the bathroom and locked me in. I was screaming for help, but no one could hear me. I smelt the smoke invade the house. I couldn't tell you how old they were or what they looked like. The fire emerged into the room. It licked my leg as if I were its prey. The next minute the fire was all over me. The window smashed from the heat and it was only then that I realised my escape route. I climbed out as best as I could and collapsed outside. When I looked down I was lying on my best friend's corpse.

Josh Taggart (12)
English International College, Málaga

A Day In The Life Of Me!

Life is one big gastronomic pleasure for me. I'm always hungry and live in hope. Let me tell you about my day. It begins like any other normal day, lots of shouting from upstairs as the sun begins to rise and so does my family. I do find it a little irritating but then again it could mean breakfast.

I lie next to my sister, who is always grooming herself, hoping that her tongue will slip and clean me. It's all just too much effort. Help! The manky mutt has just chased me up the stairs trying to grab my pride and joy. Suddenly I'm alert, someone is walking towards my food bowl. Right up we get, off we go … Blimey that was tiring, but well worth it.

Sleeping is splendid, that is until you hear, 'Rupee baby, darling.' That's Mummy Meacham crooning. When she looks at me I try to escape but she comes closer, scoops me up squeezing and kissing me. I don't really agree with all this affection stuff. Finally I'm free! I need to rest. Oh please manky creature stop barking and throwing your bone at me. No, I don't want to play, leave me alone. That's a good boy.

I may leave fluff all round the house but really I'm no trouble. All I need is tuna and a cosy sofa. Oh and by the way, I'm a cute, cunning cat.

I'm so tired so that's me done for the day.

Georgia Meacham (12)
English International College, Málaga

A Boy And His Gnome

Tom was a young boy of 12 years. He was a very lonely boy with no friends. He had one member of his family left and that was his gran. Tom and his gran were very close but his gran was a bit deaf and was asleep most of the time. She stayed in her armchair all of the time. Tom and his gran were very poor. They had no money and lived in a miniscule, one-bedroomed bungalow.

Tom spent all of his time in his garden talking to his gnome. He had done this for 5 years, since his parents had died in a car crash. Tom always asked his gnome questions but never got a reply, until one day, when he was talking casually to his gnome, something amazing happened …

'I wish that I could go to another world and see other places, like a holiday,' Tom whispered.

Tom jumped when he heard his gnome answer, 'You can young boy.'

Tom rushed to speak again, 'When?'

'Now, just touch my hand.'

Tom reached out to his mini hand. He suddenly felt a rushing sensation. Ten seconds later he was in a totally different world. 'Why didn't you tell me about this place before?' asked Tom.

'I needed to know that you wouldn't tell anyone,' the gnome replied.

The city was gigantic - you couldn't see the end of it and it was full of cute little gnomes. There were baby gnomes and dog gnomes, and they were all so cute. It was a very noisy city and full of purple buildings. They walked into a shop and Tom had to shuffle along the floor like an army man. Once they'd entered Tom's jaw dropped …

Emily Rickard (12)
English International College, Málaga

The Girl Next Door

Jake lives next door to a girl called Patricia. He has lived next to her for 10 years and Jake is now 15. Jake always thought that she was a nice girl, but not much to look at. The problem for Jake was that Patricia loved him and kept looking at him in a way that he thought was strange. They went to the same school, Swordcroft School.

It was a normal day for Jake, going to school, attending classes and having normal break time, but there was one thing that he couldn't understand. Why was Patricia ignoring him? Jake had taken her for granted all these years and now she didn't seem interested in him. Jake didn't like it and he didn't know why. It seemed that he actually had feelings for her. So Jake decided to take more interest in her. He offered to carry her bags, help her in lessons and take her for a quiet drink after school.

Patricia had planned this the whole time and her tactics were working. She was pulling the fly into the spider's web and now she knew that Jake had started to like her. She now knew the next step that Jake was going to take. He was going to ask her out.

Patricia couldn't wait until the next day. School started and the first break came. She saw the boy of her dreams walk up to her looking nervous.

'Hi Patricia,' murmured Jake with fear.

'Morning Jake,' replied Patricia confidently.

'Would you like to go out this weekend to the cinema?' whispered Jake timidly.

'I would love to,' she said wrapping her arms around him.

Max Lonsdale (12)
English International College, Málaga

Alien Automatons Attack America

Last night robots from another planet landed on a popular avenue in California, USA.

The spaceship sent from California four weeks ago had crash landed on their planet and disturbed them. The aliens had then taken the spaceship and locked the new autopilot system to the co-ordinates where it had been sent from.

The robots were commanded by their alien leader and avidly took to destroy our city, bent on revenge. Four people have already been found dead, over $1,000,000 worth of buildings have been destroyed and the robots have taken a bus with around 30 people on it hostage.

The president had a meeting on the matter and a military general said that they should attack them with fire power. But George Bush was averse to the idea because they weren't fully sure how much destructive power the aliens had.

A local passer-by, who was at the scene when the aliens crashed said, 'I was just walking my dog when it all happened. Before it landed my dog was acting weird as if he knew something was happening'.

Another man, whose name we can't reveal for legal reasons said, 'The spaceship was massive, bigger than The White House. It was kind of in the shape of a boomerang with lights flashing in every direction. It was a terrifying yet gobsmacking encounter'.

We still don't know what the aliens want or what will happen if they don't get it.

Rory Williamson (12)
English International College, Málaga

A Day In The Life Of David Beckham

I have just woken up. My head is spinning. I think I had too much to drink last night. I can hear the hairdryer buzzing and the kids screaming. What do I do? I want to go back to sleep. I get out of bed and go downstairs. I can see Brooklyn punching Romeo and Cruz screaming in his cot wanting to be picked up and loved. I just sit down on the sofa and try to relax. Now Brooklyn is playing football with Romeo nicely outside in the garden. At least now it's a little bit quieter.

Victoria has finished doing her hair and Cruz has now finished screaming. The house is quiet at last. All I can hear are the birds singing and the bees buzzing. Oh no, Romeo has tripped over the ball and has landed in the paddling pool. Victoria is going to kill me, he is in his new Calvin Klein trousers and shirt. This is meant to be my day off, I wasn't planning on being a nanny, if I was I would have woken up earlier and would have got dressed into my apron, not my Gucci suit.

I need to get out of the house and let my head chill for a bit. At the moment I haven't the time for wives or kids, the only thing which is on my mind is football. I feel like my life is trapped in a cage with screaming kids and an annoying wife. That's what it feels like as soon as I walk through the big, wooden front door.

Alex Pemberton (12)
English International College, Málaga

A Day In The Life Of A Teacher

9.00 The school bell goes and my nerves start shaking because my first class is ILTS. They're my worst class, they vandalise my classroom and give me attitude.

9.10 I told them to get their books out but once again they didn't listen. They just sat down shouting, so I told them all that if they didn't behave I'd send them to the headmaster, so that finally shut them up.

9.50 At last they had left and thankfully my next class was my best, ZTW. They are nice, they don't shout or scream, they just sit and listen.

10.40 It was break and the morning was over and I could relax. I was thinking of how I was going to keep Year 8 from giving me hell.

11.00 Year 8 came in with mischievous faces I already knew that it was hard to keep them quiet. Somehow they were nice, even though I had them twice.

13.00 It was my last class and they were murder. They kept on shouting but I finally saw through it.

Bye,
Mr Allen.

Joshua Kortekaas-Allen (11)
English International College, Málaga

The Box

It was early morning at the crack of dawn. Sheila had found a box. She didn't know what to do with it, she'd also found a note saying: 'Don't open this box, from me to you, you will suffer, your family too'.

She looked around, she was the only one there outside her house but she felt like someone was watching her every movement. She picked the box up, turned around and walked into her house, closing the door after her and she put the box on the table.

She looked at the box and as she kept staring at it many old faces appeared screaming for help. She tried to help them but she couldn't reach them. She looked away and then looked back at the box and the faces had disappeared. The box had a lock on it but it also had a symbol on it. It was some sort of a sign. The box was white and black, and when she looked at it, it reminded her of her dad because he did magic and he could make anything disappear. She looked at it again and she wondered what was in the box. She said, 'That's it, I'm opening it.' She pulled the lock off and opened the box. 'Argh! It hurts, get it off,' said Sheila …

Matthew Gladwell (12)
English International College, Málaga

How Day Became Night

One day God decided He wanted to settle down to rest, but should He go to Heaven or to Hell? He thought He ought to let them decide, so following His wishes, they organised a meeting to discuss it. The meeting went badly. Hell wasn't compromising. They wanted Him so much; they would give up or do anything to get Him. To Hell this meant war!

What Hell didn't know was that while they were planning their war to destroy Heaven, the head angel persuaded God to rest in Heaven for eternity. When Hell found out they were furious. So they decided to take revenge by planning a method of attack. Their idea was to torture Earth because of Heaven taking God. Earth would have famine and live in darkness. The question was would they succeed?

The head angel was wise and aware of their evil. So she made an escape plan, to save the Earth and to keep Heaven in existence. Hell made it more difficult by switching from one half of the world to the other, so it was impossible for Heaven to catch them. The head angel could only keep half the world alight for 14 hours and so the battle continues.

This is how day becomes night.

Sophie Leaver (12)
English International College, Málaga

A Day In The Life Of An Ordinary Cat

One day I was being chased by the neighbour's dog and I turned left to go under the fence, which was my usual route, when suddenly I ran straight into the fence with a *thud!* Someone had covered my hole up. As I tried regaining my senses I saw the bounding dog speed around the corner, charging straight at me with its slobbering slimy tongue hanging out of its mouth.

I started looking for another way out when suddenly I did something amazing, I managed to leap on top of the fence. I wondered if it was only the adrenaline pumping through me or if finally I had become fit enough to jump onto it. But I had no time to sit and ponder because the beast of a dog started headbutting the fence. I grabbed on for dear life, but no use, I toppled straight off onto the other side. Whoever said cats always land on their feet must have never seen me falling off a fence. I landed with a huge crack, straight onto my back.

I slowly stood up in agony and tried crawling back to my house, which was just across the road. I thought I'd made it but on the front lawn sat one of my owners, little Timmy the baby. The chaos erupted, he pulled my tail, I screeched, his mother ran out, picked us up, put him to bed and gave me a bowl of milk. Aah! Heaven.

Tommy Walsh (12)
English International College, Málaga

A Day In The Life Of Katie Price

I have just come back from another day's hard work in London. My agent has told me that in six days I'm going to go to Dubai to do a shoot for maternity wear. Peter is shooting a new video for his new song in four days. I'm worried because there is nobody here to look after Harvey and he needs extra special care.

I'm going to get ready to go out now but I don't know what colour Juicy tracksuit to wear. I can't wait until I can wear mini skirts again after I've had my baby. After I had Harvey, I lost the weight pretty quickly.

Oh no, Harvey's crying again. I think he's hungry. I'll be back in a minute.

Time to get ready for tonight. Oh, there's the doorbell. My make-up artist and hairdresser must be here to help me get ready. I'll just go to answer the door.

Peter's going to a film premier and then he's joining me at the party.

At last I'm ready and my car and chauffeur have just turned up to drop me there.

Luckily my mother has just turned up to look after Harvey. It's 9.30pm and the party starts at 10pm. I think I'm going to be late but it's fashionable, isn't it?

I have arrived and already there are lots of people crowding me, asking me how I feel about having another baby. I'm worried about my stomach and everybody staring. I'm not going to drink anything because of the condition I'm in. The party is really good so far and they are playing loud music. I've just met Victoria and David. They look really awesome tonight. I'm going now, I better get some rest.

Phoebe Feld (12)
English International College, Málaga

The Box

It was a normal day just before the dawn broke out. Stella found a mysterious little box with ribbons covering it like a present. It was lying on the floor in her bedroom.

She looked at the golden box. It had some ancient writing on it, more or less like a warning. It said, 'Open it, I dare you'. Stella was starting to get goosebumps. She opened the horrendous little box and a white, sharp, almost blinding light appeared. All of a sudden it turned off. Nothing happened. It was empty. Then out of nowhere a mysterious deep voice said, 'You have now unleashed an everlasting curse! Ha, ha, ha!'

Stella was shocked. Her heart beat so loud - *bump, bump, bump*. She was terrified. She broke down in tears and fell asleep.

Then she had a nightmare. She was swimming with her friends. All of a sudden her friends were gone. She was all alone. The pool was calm and quiet, but then out of the waves a huge fin came to the surface. She had a small cut which started bleeding. A huge monster appeared underneath her. It bit her. It was a great white shark. She tried to escape but her foot was pulled down. It was terrible.

She woke up. Argh! She broke into tears. She was sweating.

The same voice from before said, 'Having fun? This is just the beginning.'

Blood was dripping from her arm - *drip, drip, drip* ...

Nick Leyden Van Amstel (12)
English International College, Málaga

The Curse

Have you ever heard of Pandora's box? Well this is a similar story that happened 200 years ago.

Jessica mumbled in the dark graveyard, thinking of her lovely old dad, which she would never see again. She saw images of her next to her dad having fun. Her dad died in a car accident. When she arrived to his tomb she saw a little brown box with beige borders, the strange box had a spell, which she read out:

'Powers that be
Join with me
To show my family
And let me see!'

The box started opening, her heart started beating faster and faster. A ghost appeared. She quickly closed the door without knowing that she'd freed her evil dad's spirit and left the good one in the box. Her dad disappeared. The box had another spell. She read it out. She got paralysed, she couldn't even blink.

The next day the police found Jessica dead on the floor, with a lighted torch pointing at the box I her hand. Doctors analysed her, but nobody knew how she'd died.

The next day her mum went to visit her tomb and saw a little brown box, would she dare to open it?

People think that this story is a myth or a legend, but keep your eyes open, because it could always happen to you.

Hind Kaddoura (11)
English International College, Málaga

The River Of Istan

As soon as I discovered this beautiful part of the stream at Istan, I wanted to stay there until dark. It was like an oasis in the suffocating heat of another summer in Andalusia. I loved how it was shaded by the enormous fig tree. I gladly took refuge. The trickling sound of this pure spring water made me relax as it ran slowly down the stream, taking away the aches and pains in my legs from the long hot walk. The different layers of water were split up by small waterfalls made of rock where the stream cascaded down.

It was like the stream had a mind of its own because when I was in the cool shade, the water felt lovely and warm. When I was in the boiling hot sun it was refreshing and quite cold. When I dipped my toes in, I could imagine being a droplet of water haphazardly flowing freely down the river, splashing onto rocks. If I were a droplet of water, I would only have a short life until I was evaporated by the boiling sun thirstily eating up any moisture from the rocks.

I lay down on the soft grass under the tree, feeling refreshed. The sunshine dappled the ground around me as the light escaped through the leaves wafting in the warm breeze. This really was the perfect end to an exciting but exhausting country climb with my classmates.

Ollie Zabell (12)
English International College, Málaga

The Golden Sword

The army waited in the golden halls of Ragnok Castle. The army's leader was called Trident. He was a sagacious man and had planned this war well. Archers at the rear, cavalry to the right, catapults to the left and swordsmen in the centre.

The Trident army waited for the Landoril army to arrive, but then in the distance they could see torches glowing and could hear horns blowing. The time had come and the stage was set. Rain was falling and darkness had shrouded the sky. The Landoril army was in place.

'Archers at the ready!' shouted Harold.

The archers pulled back their bowstrings, arrows slight. Suddenly an old villager let loose a flaming arrow into the colossal troll.

'So the war has begun,' shouted Harold. 'Fire!'

The arrows flew through the air straight at the centre of the Landoril army. The Landoril archers fired back knocking some men off the wall.

'Stand fast!' shouted Harold.

The Landoril scum had put ladders up against the walls. Harold's army was being overwhelmed by the might of the Landoril army. The gate was breached, all was lost.

Harold, with all his might, cut his way through the Landoril army. Suddenly a brilliant light shone on the hill, at once Harold's hopes were up. It was the army of the dead. The army of the dead swiftly slaughtered all of the Landoril army.

'Your job is done here,' Harold explained.

George Gibson (11)
English International College, Málaga

A Day In The Life Of Paris Neptune

Hi, I'm Isabella Cortez and I live in a village, a very small village, a boring, dull village. No one ever comes to our village, *ever*. That's why I was surprised when a girl moved in next door, Paris Neptune. I have been her friend for a few days now and I've noticed that she is too glamorous to fit into the village. She is too great to be here. So I've come up with an idea, I'm going to write a day in the life of Paris Neptune.

Every morning in school she is always telling stories of where she has been like Italy and Spain - really glamorous places.

Then in lessons she always puts her hand up and gets the answer right and all the boys are in love with her. They say she's pretty, she's not, she's *gorgeous*. It's so unfair.

Anyway, in sports she is the best at everything except running, she can't run but apart from that she is very much perfect.

After school she does activities when she gets home. She watches the TV with her perfect family and then goes to her bed. Her bedroom is on the other side to mine so I can hear everything. Sometimes I hear her crying. She wants to see her friends again. I wish I could help, but I don't know what to do. Poor perfect Paris!

Paige Hopkins (12)
English International College, Málaga

A Day In The Life Of Bubble The Fish

I've just woken up. I had a most peaceful sleep, still and quiet, just how I like it. Today I'm going to do what I normally do, swim, swim, eat and swim some more, swimming away all day long. This is my beautiful home, lovely blue shiny stones. I love to suck up the stones and spit them out again, I know it makes my family laugh! Green plants to swim around, crystal clear water, well most of the time, when they remember to clean my tank.

Someone will come down to feed me soon I hope. It is hungry work, sleeping and swimming. Fantastic, here's Sam, give me more of the yellow flakes, they are my favourite.

Sam always comes down before anyone else. Then Robbie, he just ignores me, and I am his really, he won me at the ferria. Then Mummy and last of all Daddy. Most days I don't see him, but oh well, sometimes I think he doesn't even know I'm alive. He thinks I have gone to the big tank in the sky with their other fish, hey not me!

They think I have a two-second memory. Well I must be a super fish, 'Bubble the Wonder Fish'. That sounds good, I like that. I remember every thing, all about my family and my life here in this tank.

Well I must say I am getting very tired now. Must be time for a sleep. Goodnight all.

Samantha Scott (12)
English International College, Málaga

A Day In The Life Of A …

I was woken up by the other giraffes as usual. This I called the rush hour because all the giraffes were hustling and bustling around like lost sheep trying to find their master. Giraffes and boars were always bumping into each other and bumping into me. I don't know why they do it. There were all so impatient, it's unbelievable.

The strange people were making silly faces at me. They looked as white as a ghost. They were looking at me like I was a nutter for not wearing clothes or something, but look at them, at least I don't spend thousands of pounds on clothes, but of course it's their choice.

As usual strange people were feeding us. When I saw a girl (I think) who had some food in her hand so I went over to get the food when she screamed into my ear because she saw my black rough tongue.

The African sun was blazing away at us on the hay. As we were taller we got more of the sun. I became tired and felt I was going to faint. So I laid down and thought that was my day finished when I heard a cry. It was that old man who took all the money. He had been hit by a boar. The man had got a spiky stick and stuck it between the boar's ears. The man had killed the boar.

I hoped this day would never happened again.

Kabir Singh Bhogal (11)
English International College, Málaga

A Day In The Life Of Barry Dawson

Again I am woken up by the screams of Mum. Frank must have gone out last night and come back drunk … again.

I hear him hitting her, screaming at her. I wish I could just leave and never come back.

I cover my ears trying to absent myself from my mum's tears and Frank's screams. I just wish none of this happens … every single day. There's nothing to stop him, he never gets enough. Eventually I go to sleep.

Sweet dreams are interrupted by the buzzing sound of my alarm clock. I go downstairs, Frank's there. He lifts his head slightly, then looks back down. 'You disgust me,' I say under my breath. He hears me. He holds me by the neck and pushes me into the wall. He laughs in my face, his breath stinking of alcohol, a sickening smell.

He begins to kick me, punch me. I cry for help. My mum rushes in to hold Frank still, but he pushes her away and she falls unconscious on the floor.

He carries on. I can't hold the tears in for any longer, they are streaming down me …

My heart is beating, my bones are sore and every breath I take is like a war to fight.

I begin to say goodbye …

If only my dad hadn't gone to work that day, he wouldn't have had the accident and died. If only my mum hadn't met Frank, none of this would be happening.

I close my eyes as I feel my heart fail. I pray for Mum. I hope she's strong, at least stronger than me.

Carmen Cuadra-Gomez (13)
English International College, Málaga

Being Me For A While

I often wonder why I'm here. I mean, what did I do wrong? I guess it doesn't matter now. She will never come back for me, not my mother. Thirteen years have passed, not a letter, or even a note. I sometimes wonder, wonder what she was like. Maybe she only left me here because she didn't have enough money and she wants to come and collect me, but she has a boyfriend now, and he said she could never see me again. Maybe I wasn't planned, her boyfriend left, she was too far into the pregnancy for an abortion. She had no choice but to have me. She was young and needed a new life away from me so she could finish school.

Sorry, I have a weird imagination. I always make up things. At school I'm like it too. I can't help it, some words come out and I just can't help myself. It's like a volcano, only erupting with words, sentences, that form stories upon stories.

My life isn't that bad, I mean, look at the place around me. The people here are so nice, they are not my mother but they treat me like I'm their child. I have been fostered with this couple for nine months.

People sometimes ask, they ask why do I think about my mother so much when I never knew her, and she hasn't ever even tried to find me? The truth is, it doesn't matter what happened, she is still my mother, my mum and nothing will change that. Even though I don't know what she looks like, or what her name is, it doesn't matter to me because she is part of me. In my head I know she did the right thing for both of us. Everything happens for a reason.

Lydia Mills (13)
English International College, Málaga

Strange Pianist

The 7th April was a strange day. That night a man was found in Sheerness wearing a tie and a suit, both soaked. All the tags had been removed from every item that he wore. The police picked him up and from that moment he hasn't spoken a word. They sent him to the mental health care centre in the north of Kent. He looked as if he were in his early 20s, or early 30s. When he was given a piece of paper and a pencil, with the hope of him writing his name, he drew a grand piano. His carers put him in front of a piano that was in the hospital chapel. He stunned them with a classical performance.

After being summated to a group of physiological tests, they found out that he was in good physical condition, therefore he could eat and drink. People said he communicated with music. One theory said that he had a great resemblance to a pianist in Italy. Even though his hair was different, his nose and facial structure were very similar. He also stayed silent. A doctor said that he thought that this man was living a normal life until 7th April and suffered a trauma. This case has many different theories but the truth is not easy to reveal.

Bilal Abou El Ela Bourquin (11)
English International College, Málaga

A Day In The Life Of Poor Little Mary

'Why didn't you run away?'

'She had me tight between her legs so I couldn't.'

'But it must have hurt so much.'

'I couldn't stop crying and that made Mummy cross.'

'Did she smack you?'

'You always get a hard smack if you cry.'

'My mum doesn't ever smack me.'

'My mummy smacks me lots. I deserve it because I'm bad,' confessed Mary.

'That's rubbish. I don't know how your mum would cope with Rochelle or Jade, or Sophie for that matter.'

'Mummy tells me I'm naughty.'

'But you're not naughty.'

'I am though Dixie, I do really dirty things,' Mary said hoarsely.

'Like what?'

'I pick my nose. I scratch myself and sometimes I don't get to the toilet in time.'

'You and everyone else in the world!'

'Mummy says I'm still dirty. Sometimes the dirt doesn't show, but Mummy says she can see it. And sometime I have to take lots of medicine so the dirt inside me can disappear.'

I stared at her blankly. 'Your Mum's nuts!' I said.

Mary looked startled. 'No she's not, she only cares about me, she says so.'

'She's worse than nuts, she's cruel,' I said, gently picking up one of Mary's tiny little hands.

'Dixie? Promise me something, don't say anything to anyone.'

'OK!'

'Yeah, sure but ...'

'But nothing Dixie, if Mummy finds out it might get worse and she might get angry, and I don't want her to get cross,' she said, crying onto my shoulder.

I feel so helpless. Mary doesn't deserve any of this - she's clever, and she's the most sweetest little girl I've ever met. If only I knew how to help, to stop this happening again.

Aishah Abdulla (14)
English International College, Málaga

A Day In The Life Of A Fly

Today was a beautiful day. Everything was perfect. I could just smell it. As I got out of bed, I immediately felt alive, awake and refreshed. First things first. Breakfast. Probably the best part of the day. I went outside to find my breakfast waiting for me on my front step. Chocolate ice cream and brownies. Yum. I sucked up everything instantly. I decided to check up on Greg. Greg was my best friend since we were tiny little naughty worms. It's been a day since … Anyway, I made my way as fast as possible, in fact, I flew there. *Bang!* Ouch! Oh, I could've guessed: The window. It's always so shiny and clean it just doesn't seem like it's actually there. I tried again. *Bang!* Dammit! Again! *Bang! Bang! Bang!* Finally I turned left and realised the other side of the window was open. Greg was on the inside of the window trying to get out.

'I hate this place! It's like a trap! Oh, hey Francis, how's it going?'

Greg. Always daydreaming. Never realises what's really happening. I think he lives in his own little world sometimes …

'I'm OK Greg. Everything's going great for me! Hey, want to get something to eat? I'm still starving!'

'OK,' replied Greg. As we were about to take off … *smack!*

That was the end of Greg's and my days as a fly.

Philippe Andre Barrage Sanchez (14)
English International College, Málaga

A Day In The Life Of Sir Alex Ferguson

7am   He slowly gets up out of his four-poster bed in the Celtic
           Manor.

7.15am   He starts getting dressed before the big day.

7.20am   He slips some headache tablets into his bag just in case
           Man U lose.

8am   He trudges down to breakfast only to find his 18 players
           playing waiters so he picks them for the match. The last
           thing he needs!

9am   Still wondering if to play Gary Neville or not, he sits down
           right at the front of the bus.

11am   Sir Alex makes the decision that Gary Neville will be on the
           bench and Wes Brown will start.

12pm   After a mix-up with the security guard, they find that their
           dressing room is being used by the referees, and stinks.

2pm   Match draws closer as Fergie starts biting his fingernails.

3pm   Man U and Arsenal kick off. Fergie puts the first of many
           chewing gums in his mouth.

3.45pm   Fergie's furious in the dressing room as his team did not
           take their chances.

3.55pm   The other players leave the changing rooms apart from
           Fergie and Rooney. He tells Rooney, 'It's your day son.'

4.10pm   Fergie shouts at Wenger, 'Your team's rubbish.'

4.30pm   Nistelrooy misses a sitter, Ferguson kicks the bench.

4.55pm   Extra time. Another chewing gum goes into the mouth of
           Ferguson - his jaw must be tired!

5.45pm   Penalties and Ferguson has the headache tablets in his
           pocket.

5.55pm   Viera scores to win Arsenal the FA Cup. Ferguson gets up
           from the bench and shakes Wenger's hand, he wants to
           throttle him.

6.10pm   All the players are shouting and blaming other people, while Fergie starts on the headache tablets.

8pm   They arrive back at the hotel. Ferguson jumps off the bus and shouts, 'Training first thing Monday morning.'

10pm   He wishes he could go back twelve hours.

Tommy Foster (13)
English International College, Málaga

The Day Of A Dog

I woke up with the opening of the door, I stretched myself out with a huge yawn. Ricardo came in and went to the fridge, opening the door and took the milk out. I jumped off the basket and followed him with tail moving continuously. He took a cup and poured it until it reached the top. I started whining, looking at him with a miserable face. I wouldn't stop until I got my food.

'OK, OK,' he said leaving the cup of milk to one side and approaching the pantry. He took the sugar and went back to his milk. I yawned even harder and then with a smile on his face went again and took out my huge dog food bag, got my bowl from the kitchen wardrobe and poured all the biscuits on the bowl. Every morning while the biscuits fall one by one on the bowl I close my eyes and listen to the biscuits hit each other in the end of the bowl, I love the sound. I eat the biscuits while Ricardo has his breakfast watching TV. Then the mean little girl comes in called Cristina with a mixture of anger and tiredness on her face. It is really funny how they fight for the remote control, I always want to see it in first row so sometimes I get in the way and end up being whacked.

Ricardo is really nice to me, but is normally not around. He always goes away with this really fast animal that rolls on the road. I try to follow him, sneaking out the gate just in time and run behind this huge animal that they call 'Car' but I always fail and go back inside.

Ricardo Bocanegra (14)
English International College, Málaga

The Dragon Could Not Breathe Fire

Once a long, long time ago lived a dragon named Drake, Drake was not a normal dragon at all, he had claws and scales but unlike all his other friends, he could not breathe fire. Then all of a sudden the *Ice Age* came all the other dragons got away because they melted the ice but Drake couldn't melt the ice, he was trapped! For thousands of years he stayed frozen in a block of ice.

200,000 years later, Drake still in the ice …

It's a normal day in New York, the shops and the market are flowing with people, until a small tremble shakes New York, this tremble is strong enough to feel but as soon as it's finished everyone goes on with their normal lives, but little did they know from that day on their lives would be far from normal. This is because that tremble is small on the land but down deep, where Drake is, it is so big it cracks the ice. Drake is trapped in, in half, immediately Drake starts clubbing up through the ground. Unluckily, as soon as Drake reaches the ground he eats 36 people, one of the people he eats was the boy writing this story. Think about it, wouldn't you be hungry after 200,000 years?

Thomas Barnes (13)
English International College, Málaga

Mini-Man

Yesterday morning in Central Park a young boy, who was going through the park on his bike, claimed that he'd seen a small man walking out of a little hole in the rocks.

The boy, 13, was interested to see who this small person was so he went over to the hole and looked inside. He said, 'It was amazing, it was like a hobbit's house. Everything was so small, the chairs, height of the doors and even the plates!'

The boy went inside the house and said that he'd seen the little man reading the newspaper which was about the size of himself. The boy approached the small man, he suddenly jumped up and started shouting in an unknown language and then started attacking the poor boy violently.

The small boy ran out of the house and asked for the help of builder, Fred Davies, 59. When they approached the small house, they witnessed the small person running out. Mr Davies, who was with the boy at the time, managed to capture a photo of the mini-man on his mobile phone.

Scientists have cordoned off the area and are investigating the claims. They are unwilling to comment at this time but have admitted to receiving other reports of aggressive miniature people.

Archie Mustafa (13)
English International College, Málaga

The Game

The sun is shining over London and all the innocent children are walking to school; their bags strung loosely over their shoulders, their mothers running behind them screaming gently that they've forgotten their lunches or reminding them that they have to get the bus that evening, they frown as their children wave it away with one hand and continue down the road to rejoin the throng of children laughing merrily to their school.

For me however, it is a totally different situation, I am not walking; I'm cruising down the street doing 80mph in a black Porsche Boxster, focusing on the task ahead. I drive up past the London Dungeons and turn right into a small car park next to a Lloyds TSB. I get out of my car making sure I've parked in view of the security camera. As I walk along the side of the bank, I look left and see my Lamborghini Gallardo is parked on the corner of the street. I then turn towards the bank and enter. I feel my pocket and make sure I've got my gun. I go over to a lady behind the counter.

'Excuse me could I withdraw some money?'

'Of course, do you have your card?'

'No, but I have this.' I take out the gun.

Within minutes I am driving down the street, in the Lamborghini, I hear sirens …

'Come on Stephen, pack up your toys.'

'But Mu- …'

'Now.'

I pack up my cars and go to bed. 'Goodnight.'

Tom Clarke (12)
European School of Luxembourg, Luxembourg

A Day In The Life Of A Dustbin

Everyone says that dustbins are dirty, ugly *things.* But without us there would be rubbish spilling out onto the streets, and flies would be buzzing everywhere, infecting the whole place and making tiny toddlers cry. But no, we're thought of as disgusting, useless objects. Between you and me, I think of humans as disgusting, useless objects. They stuff mouldy chips and rotting vegetables into me, and then slam my head back onto my body without caring that I'm going to get a searing headache later. Let me tell you a little story to explain …

It was a chilly October evening, and I was just standing outside a house, minding my own business, when out of the shadows crept two figures, dressed all in black. Their faces were hidden with masks, and they were tiptoeing along. I knew at once that something fishy was going on, with something I like to call 'dustbin intuition'. And as the twosome passed me, I realised that they were robbers! Instantly, I started rocking back and forth, making as much noise as I could. The robbers stared at me in surprise, and then glanced up to the window of the house where a woman, holding a phone, now stood. Then came the police sirens, and soon enough both the robbers were being handcuffed. They were led away, and after a while, the commotion died down. Who says the life of a dustbin isn't interesting?

Sarah Graham (12)
European School of Luxembourg, Luxembourg

A Day In the Life Of …

Here I am basking in the sun with a dog peeing against my leg. Thank goodness that smelly tramp has left; his awful stink is finally wearing off.

This morning two lovers stopped to rest. The man was called Tom and the woman, Kate. Tom made a long emotional speech which lasted for about ten minutes. Finally he asked Kate for her hand in marriage. After a lot of crying and fuss, she said yes. They kissed with joy, I could feel the happiness bouncing off the engaged couple. They walked away hand in hand.

Then a woman and her one-year-old child, whose scream sounded like a bird getting squashed, stopped by. My goodness what a racket! In all my years, I have never heard a baby scream so loudly. The baby only shut up when he saw a little dog coming down the path. He pulled the poor creature's tail, the dog yelped out in pain and bit the baby's hand, and rightly so. I personally blame the parents. The embarrassed mother walked away with her deafening baby.

Goodness gracious me, those children really think that they are the best, don't they? They have absolutely no respect for the world around them. One cheeky runt sprayed me with this foul-smelling, bright pink paint. On top of that, I am covered in bird droppings.

Oh well, tomorrow I will be repainted and once again I will become the spotless, first class park bench I used to be.

Emily Simpson (12)
European School of Luxembourg, Luxembourg

Genghis Khan's Horse

Genghis Khan was a happy man. And why shouldn't he be? He was Supreme Ruler of Central Asia, blessed with strong healthy sons, a loyal loving wife and thousands of fellow nomadic warriors to starve and even die for him. Above all, his greatest joy was his horse which he fondly called Lightning.

But alas, Lightning the horse dropped dead from fatigue during one of the Great Khan's military expeditions. This posed a problem for the Great Khan's tribe, the Borujins (translated as sons of the wolf). Now you shouldn't be fooled by the Khan's over-muscular build, stern glare and ruthless reputation, he was really just an old softie and so he shed tears a-many over his beloved four-legged companion's tragic demise. The Khan, being extremely insecure, had already been attending a renowned therapist in the area to try to help him deal with this problem and now this sense of insecurity was multiplied as the great Khan superstitiously believed that a Mongol warrior was powerless without a horse and so with his companion's body now four feet under the Earth, he lost all confidence in commanding his troops to plunder and pillage.

The great Khan's friend at the local coffee shop saw a solution. After a round of sour horse milk, the latter proclaimed to the Khan that all he should do is buy a new horse. The great Khan commented that it was a most agreeable idea.

The next morning the Khan went with his wife to purchase a horse.

'Oh honey!' he wailed. 'Why did you have to come with me? All the guys at the coffee shop will think I'm a wimp attached to his wife's apron strings!'

'Oh do shut up!' replied his spouse, twirling her dark wavy hair. 'Last horse you bought dropped dead. Our family horse needs to be reliable, spacious and economical, not just flashy and fast like that no good Lightning.'

'Hey, don't talk about my deceased friend like that,' growled Genghis Khan, 'woman!' he added briskly.

'What did you say?'

'Oh, nothing!'

The horse dealer at the shop was an Uzbek. He was a short stocky man with deep-set hazel eyes which gleamed at the sight of gold coins. The dealer was rather surprised to see Genghis Khan. After all, the Khan was rumoured by the local tabloids to have been preparing for an invasion of India.

'Oh Mighty Khan, what brings you down to good old Smarkend?' enquired the dealer. 'Mrs Khan, what's a fine lady like you doing in a place like this?' he added, chortling at his stale humour. 'Is it a horse you're looking for?'

'You're a ray of sunshine, aren't you?' Mrs Khan proclaimed, rolling her almond-shaped eyes.

'Yes, yes, my last horse died and I need to buy another one so I can make it on a big plundering raid of Delhi before the summer holidays.'

'Well come right in then. Our horses are the finest you'll see in all of Turkestan.'

Making a choice was arduous, especially under the picky eye of Mrs Khan, but at last …

'Oh I like this one!' pointed Mrs Khan at a proud, white stallion and clapping her hands.

'Oh what refined taste you have madame!' noted the Uzbek sycophantically. 'This one's one of our finest specimens. It's all the way from the plains of Northern Kazakhstan, just by the Altay Mountains, a region famous for its production of top quality horses. This one can do 0-20 miles in under 17 seconds. Notice how shiny and soft its coat is? There's plenty of room for the kids at the back. If you want we can …'

'I don't care from what plains it came. It may as well have been mass-bred in China. All I care about is its energy consumption,' Mrs Khan interrupted.

'Only 10 carrots a day!' said the horse dealer proudly.

'Well, I don't know!' exclaimed Genghis Khan sceptically. 'It's not as fast as Lightning was!'

'We'll take it!' bellowed Mrs Khan, giving her husband a piercing look which suggested this was an ultimatum.

The Khans christened the horse Thunder. The Great Khan learned to love the horse. The plundering raid went well enough! The Great Khan had never felt better in his life. Then Thunder the horse got food poisoning and died.

'You know what, I think I'll just walk from now on!' said the Great Khan.

His companion at the local coffee shop had to agree.

Halil Halil (16)
Falcon School, Cyprus

A Day In The Life Of An Animal

My hooves thudded hard on the ground and my heart raced as I ran across the field. This was it! This was my escape!

'Oi! What's that crazy stallion got up to now Jimmy? He's heading for the fence!' shouted James.

'What? Saddle the horses James.'

The chase was up. I heard the men galloping at full speed. I approached the fence and made a great leap over it. I threw my head up high, shaking my inky black mane to and fro and ran like an arrow. The sun began to sink into the horizon, like a colossal red ball.

'Jimmy, let's go back. It's gettin' dark,' mumbled James.

'What, you a coward James?' replied Jimmy sharply. 'I'm not going back till I get me that horse, y'hear?'

'Look, the horse'll probably lie down to rest.'

As I descended a hill, I spotted my pursuers meandering in the dusk. I galloped aimlessly and sought refuge at a nearby barn.

'Have you Sir, by any chance, seen a stallion around these parts?' Jimmy questioned the owner.

'No Sir.'

'Y'sure?'

'Sure I am.'

'C'mon Jimmy, let's go. He says there ain't no horse here,' mumbled James hurriedly.

The moon filtered in the barn gently, casting shadows on the straw. I stood in silence watching James and Jimmy ride off in a cloud of dust. Who knew what tomorrow might bring. I was safe for the moment!

Natasha Holmes (14)
Falcon School, Cyprus

Sing Mockingbird, Sing

Screams were heard from everyone. Arthur never wanted to fight but he was forced to for the protection of his home town. He had heard terrifying tales about wars where children fought for the rights of their people, where innocent people were slaughtered by heartless soldiers.

He was placed in a troop of soldiers, commanded by General Torns. He never obeyed his commands if they included murdering children, families or the elderly. Instead, he rescued the enemy's citizens and sneaked them into a wooden house, a day's journey from Naut but Arthur never rode with them. As an alternative he sent them to a friend of his who guided them to safety.

The sky was grey from the smoke of the fireballs the armies of Bertroth and Naut were throwing. The ground was cold but they had a duty to fulfil and so they proceeded to fight.

The King of Naut wore heavy armour, a massive sword by his side and rode steadily on his pitch-black horse. He slowly approached Bertroth's King and they began to fight.

The fight lasted for over an hour and it seemed they were both winning but they grew weaker by every second. The King of Bertroth would never surrender his beautiful and prosperous town.

Finally the endless fighting between what seemed to be good and evil was over, after seven years of battle when the King of Bertroth killed the King of Naut by piercing his stomach with his sharp sword.

Daria Kolmogorova (12)
Falcon School, Cyprus

A Day In The Life Of My Fat Cat

Correction: My *very* fat cat, as in Guinness Book of Records fat. I can't lift her anymore. She's very vicious, which intimidates me despite her size. Her name is Whiskey. Yes, after the drink. Her fur is a light brown and her eyes are light blue. We recently obtained a fridge magnet which says:

> *'It's really the cat's house,*
> *We just pay the mortgage'.*

Just another morning. I stretched out on my mat outside the back door. I could hear one of the humans opening the door. Mornings meant ham. Every morning one of the humans would take out the ham. Usually I got a few pieces. It fed me my first meal. Satisfied, I went to my couch where I slept every morning and afternoon. Sleepy time. Already all this excitement had worn me out.

When I woke up again the sun was shining brightly. I waited for the humans to come home. Later one of the humans brought the dogs in. Those pesky dogs. Inside was mine, outside they could have. If any of them ventured close, they got some claws to teach them. They knew by now that I meant business. I knew their tricks.

The sun was gone now. My last meal was fed to me. Yes! Tuna today.

The sky turned black. Back to the doorstep again. Those stupid dogs would settle down. Don't they understand that I need my beauty sleep? Dogs! So stupid.

Noeleen Advani (13)
Falcon School, Cyprus

Hide-And-Seek

I took a deep breath as I rounded another curve in the path. I remembered the village myth and all the neighbours' words of warning. Once again I had rebelled against them, just to feel the thrill of danger and my blatant oblivion. I always did that. A kind of sickness I inhabited, to get a better taste of life … so I thought.

I could no longer see the tall rusting iron gate which played the doorway to the surroundings of this forbidden zone. It was so barren of all living things and everything seemed so distorted, like a dream. I had been hiding for too long and my breathing had got too heavy to handle, which is why I had decided to make a move. If I hadn't, who knows what would have happened to me in that hiding place. Its surrounding vaporous backdrop would have come in the terror of the moment and clasped me into a void along with it. I had been hidden, yet so exposed. I was also so very sure that *she* was not a figment of my imagination. I could feel her. Even now as I was running, *she* was advancing on me slowly and getting closer with every breath lost. I was running away from it all. All of the things I had wanted to see in this place for so long. Running away from the princess of the myth. As I ran, thoughts bounded through my head. *Where was everyone? Surely they would have known that the game would be over by now.* My breathing was stunted and abrupt and sweat trickled down my cheeks, the little beads racing one another. As I ran, I filled the dusty path with clues - my footprints.

'Anyone up for hide-and-seek in the graveyard?'

The comment that had been shouted by one of the neighbourhood children that evening, after supper. We had all jumped at the idea. Myth or no myth, now it seemed so stupid. Suddenly my body froze without warning. *She … it …* was now right behind me. So close that I could feel her iciness dampening my already shrivelled skin. *She* breathed, I dare not. There was no way of hiding now … besides, the game had long finished.

Tara Tate (15)
Falcon School, Cyprus

A Day In The Life Of A Rabbit

I skip across a newly cut lawn, fascinated by each individual blade of grass tickling my furry, round tummy. My whiskers twitch and I nibble contentedly on herbs and clover. I hear a noise but it is merely a sparrow, singing in an effortless monotone trill.

Today the weather is fine and since foxes and other beasts are scarce, this enhances the dream-like quality of the day. And yet this lack of predators makes me feel sorrowful and I grieve at the thought of our cousins; the winter rabbits, who once raged a vicious war against mankind and the carnivores, intending to drive them from our society. And so, on this present day, the winter rabbits are banished from residences and driven out of meadows, fearing hawks, foxes and owls.

My mother will be hopping mad when I return to my burrow, as she has warned me countless times how dangerous it is outside during the day. I prance, leaping in the grass; another day in the life of a rabbit.

But now I feel a hard surface beneath my feet. Then I hear a loud buzzing noise, mounting to a vexing whine. I flush readily; the irritating beat beneath my feet becomes louder. An F1 racer shoots by.

The rabbit is annihilated in a cloud of blood, guts and bone. Its fresh sodden entrails exploded onto the side of the racetrack.

A day in the life of a rabbit, unfortunately.

Nicholas Papaxanthos (14)
Falcon School, Cyprus

A Bittersweet Adventure

'Bye, we'll miss you loads, email me every day,' wept my best friend, Lyla. I gave her one last hug, yelled goodbye to my friends and climbed into the taxi, next to my father.

'Sweetie, it's not the end of the world,' he tried to comfort me.

'It is to me,' I replied bitterly.

Well, bye-bye London, where the last fourteen years of my life I had lived a comfortable and luxurious life, surrounded by friends and family. And 'hello!' Uige, Angola. I was still shocked how my father could have done this to me: the Marburg virus, which is closely related to Ebola and is one of the world's deadliest viral diseases, had broken out in Uige, where it is thought that hunters came into contact with infected dead green monkeys. So my father, a noted epidemiologist, had decided to volunteer and put his skills to use there. I admired that but to tear me away from my life, to drag me along with him, I couldn't.

I spent the rest of the plane ride thinking about how furious I was at my inconsiderate father and ignoring him every time he tried to approach me.

The first thing that hit me when I got off the plane was the sweltering heat so I fanned myself with a brochure my dad had given me to try and interest me in Angola. We were in a taxi with no windows, sagging seats and faulty air conditioning with a humorous, jolly taxi driver who chatted in Bantu, completely oblivious to the fact that we couldn't understand anything. Suddenly my father's mobile rang and after he'd hung up, he asked if we could stop by the hospital - one of the patients had become delirious - one of the symptoms of late Marburg, along with liver failure and multi-organ dysfunction. I replied, 'Sure, it's not like I have anything better to do.'

From the outside, the hospital looked relatively new but when we got inside, I was shocked and overwhelmed with compassion for these poor people. The stench inside the cramped ward was so nauseating but I fought the impulse to gag and to back out of the door.

I then realised the move had nothing to do with me, the feeble patients were powerless against this disease and my father was their only remnant of hope.

'Oh Daddy ...'

Olympia Severis (14)
Falcon School, Cyprus

A Day In The Life Of A Cat

It was 6.30 in the morning and the private cats' meeting was about to begin.

'Quiet everyone, quiet ...' The voices died down as we listened to the chief - 'Mr X' they call him. Nobody knows his real name but they all fear him and respect him, no one ever dares to outsmart him.

'Now we all know why we're here today on such short notice, we have a major problem with the dogs of the city. Their chief has declared a war against us and claims that he will tear us apart. Hmf! Dogs, what do they know? They're as worthless as cockroaches! They're not even worthy of their three letter name. But us, we're different, we were born to rule the world and our name - cats, is only the name others know us by, but they don't know our real, complicated name - cataromolicafs.'

He carried on and on about how important cats are to the world and explained that he was going to form a plan to defeat the dogs. I went back home to find my stupid owner, as she calls herself, still asleep. I jumped onto her bed and started purring until she woke up and poured me a bowl of milk. I drank it and left the house to meet up with Tony, the next-door neighbour's cat.

'Heya there Falafel, have you seen Tony?' What a stupid name, Falafel! He was Tony's best friend.

'Mornin' pal, yeah I've seen him, he went to search for yous, but I see he didn't find ya.'

'Okay, thanks Falafel, do you mind if I hang around with you for a while till my man Tony comes?'

'No problemo. So, how'd the meetin' go? Was it about the dogs again? Those filthy mutts!'

'Yeah about the dogs, but this time Mr X has a plan, he said he'll tell us later tonight.'

'That guy's the best, he'll probably come up with a plan that's so good, we'll crush those dogs.'

'Well, we'll just have to wait and see, anyways I think I'm gonna go look for Tony now, see ya around!'

'See ya buddy!' he called after me.

I decided to forget about Tony and go and have a nap instead; I slept for about three hours and got up in the late afternoon. I found something to eat and again went to see Tony, this time I found him. We talked about Mr X and the dogs and decided to go mouse hunting. We caught one but we didn't eat it because I was full and he said that the thing looked too skinny.

At around 7, we went back to the secret meet-up spot for cats and again Mr X gave us a long speech. However, he said that there could be a dog around listening and that he would send each of us a personal assistant of his to tell us privately the plan.

Unfortunately, I couldn't stay about long enough; I had to report straight to Dr Gollerto at 8 sharp. Dr Gollerto is my boss, chief of the dogs and I am his undercover agent.

Sama Meibar (14)
Falcon School, Cyprus

The Buddy

He moved stealthily, barely making any sound and yet was always alert. He knew that even to be heard was a crime in his profession. The loud crackle of a twig underneath him made him halt very abruptly. A bead of perspiration slid down his forehead as he strained to hear for anyone approaching. Careful not to make any more sound, he wiped his brow and carried on crouching as he went.

As soon as he reached the site, he knew how simple his task was and yet every man who tried it always failed. The person he had to meet with his buddy was notoriously known as 'Karlos the Krow', but to him names and professions did not matter.

As he helped his faithful buddy get ready for the big job, he realised how useless he would be without his buddy. Like a hacker without his computer or a soldier without his gun. But his buddy was no tool - he was his friend, his assistant.

An hour later Karlos appeared, surrounded by half a dozen men, but still clearly visible to him and his buddy. Very slowly he helped his buddy up and pulled. His buddy shuddered very gently.

Suddenly it was as if time had slowed down and he could see everything so clearly. He enjoyed this part about his job the most. The object his buddy had released moved like a stone moves through water - slowly and yet with a determined effort to reach the bottom. He could feel vibrations from where it had left and could see small ripples surrounding it. As it neared Karlos, everything came back to real time and as he turned and ran, holding on to his buddy tightly, he heard someone falling.

Twenty-four hours later at Santiago Airport he read a newspaper proclaiming the title:- 'Suspected Drug Baron Assassinated'.

Smiling to himself he walked to his gate, lovingly thinking of his buddy concealed in a fishing rod case and knowing how useless he would be as a sniper without his buddy.

Apoorv Bhargava (15)
Falcon School, Cyprus

The Final Clue

Sweat trickled down her black tailored suit as Margaret took her place amongst the crowd of people lining up in front of the white door.

She was panting with exhaustion and her face was plastered with a look of anxiety and horror. A feeling of loss was lurking in the back of her senses yet she couldn't recall what it was that had left her feeling like this. Squashed like a pearl amongst the soft interiors of an oyster is how she felt standing between a chubby middle-aged American woman and a large old man, wrinkled and barely standing as he was unable to carry his own weight.

Unaware of her situation, Margaret slowly made sense of her surroundings. There she was amongst people from all walks of life and as she peered over the row of heads, all she could make out was this monumental white door.

In a moment of puzzlement Margaret's mind drifted back to her teenage years and she remembered how she and her friends used to stand in a line in front of a white door clothed in flirty dresses and wedges as high as skyscrapers. Back then it was to go clubbing, but now, Margaret had no idea where she was.

All around her Margaret could hear an indistinct murmur as the people standing in the line conversed. Margaret, keeping to her diffident nature, spoke to no one and as time passed and more and more people entered through the white door, Margaret got closer and closer.

Several hours passed but to Margaret it felt like eternity as if time was stretching. Margaret's time finally came when the chubby middle-aged American woman disappeared behind the door. Margaret stepped up.

All of Margaret's feelings were centred around confusion, 'Where was she?' A light then shone on her with rays of translucent yellow capturing the facets of the jewels on Margaret's wedding ring, reflecting broken shards of light on the door. That's when it dawned on her. Her wedding ring. Her car accident with her husband Bernard. The old man standing in line with her. The white door.

Margaret was a woman who had never liked to question life yet there was one question she'd always asked Bernard. Death. What came next?

Her answer was finally granted. Margaret was knocking on Heaven's door.

Romy Wakil (16)
Falcon School, Cyprus

The Glass People

Trying to sleep, the only thing I could think of was that boy. I wanted to be his friend, I really did, but there was something evil in those dark, sullen eyes of his. I didn't quite know what it was … until earlier that night.

He was sitting alone on the bench next to the vacant swings, stone-like and possibly dead. I was studying him from a good distance away and not once did he flinch, not even when that bully Earl Carno threw an empty pack of cigarettes at his head. If I hadn't seen the rest, I would have definitely thought he was dead. The boy didn't even blink. Earl stopped short of his tracks and looked at his mates, another sad couple of seventeen-year-old 'rebels'.

I knew something bad was going to happen. I could hear it. Carno and his friends were circling his bench, hitting him on the head and shouting insults at him. One of them even smashed an empty bottle of vodka on the ground in front of the boy and I heard the shards fall like tinkles of a Christmas carol.

If only people were made of glass, I thought bitterly.

I felt sorry for him but what was I supposed to do? Help! I was a bit too young to die. I'm not quite sure what happened next because my head began to feel light and my vision was blurry. Seeing the flight was like trying to see the world through a needle hole and I thought I was having a seizure. But from what I could make out, the boy's face was changing … for the worst. It looked like an invisible flame was melting his skin and revealing the sick, blue scaly interior. Carno and his gang were frozen in absolute terror (as was I) and it was only when the 'boy' arched his back and thick spikes of bone pierced through his skin, that the first scream ripped through the air like a nine inch blade through linen. The mutant-thing opened its mouth and a black serpent's tongue shot out and wrapped itself around Carno's beefy neck with a sickening slap and his face hissed and sizzled as acid sprayed out of its four-jawed mouth. One tried to run away but the mutant lashed out its tail at him and sliced it clean through him; his body divided and slipped apart. Before the last guy could even react, the mutant pounced on him and his screams were cut short.

I ran and ran, all the way home, throwing up several times along the way, screaming like a madman. It was only in the safety of my bed that I realised that I had finally found someone different … like me.

Gary-Thomas Aspell (16)
Falcon School, Cyprus

Samurai Jin Kazama

Once upon a time there lived a brave Japanese samurai warrior called Jin Kazama, who was on a quest to destroy the evil demon called Heihachi. On his quest, Jin was accompanied by his best friend, Hwoarang. Baek Doo San, his master, gave Jin the Soulcalibur, the sword that could kill Heihachi. Jin and Hwoarang went through many perils and dangers and finally reached Heihachi's 'Castle of Doom'.

Jin knew Heihachi was in the castle. They quietly went to the main entrance and sliced the guards' heads off and entered the castle. When they entered the castle, suddenly from thin air Heihachi appeared.

Heihachi looked like a really muscly human being with thin red eyes. Heihachi saw the Soulcalibur in Jin's hand and got a little frightened. So Heihachi sent out a killing laser from his eyes towards Jin, but Hwoarang came in front of Jin and took it on himself and died. Jin got very furious and so ran towards Heihachi and when Heihachi went to attack, Jin jumped over him and from behind him sliced his legs off. It was not that bad for Heihachi to have no legs because using his powers he could float in mid-air. Heihachi punched Jin with his rock-solid fists. Jin fell to the ground helpless and with blood flowing out of his mouth. Jin quickly got up and put the Soulcalibur through Heihachi's heart, which killed him. So after that time, the world never knew any evil.

Anurag Rekhal (12)
Falcon School, Cyprus

Jaeger

He woke from the sand falling onto his face. He opened his eyes first, he did not know where he was, but fast, too fast, the memories came back. He was in a trench in the area of Ypern, on the allied side. He got up with the thought hammering in his brain: *No west wind, no west wind, no west wind.* He looked over the top of the trench and the wind blew sand into his face. West wind.

They had to strike today. They had waited so long, now they had their wind for a gas attack. And he sat in the trench opposite the German lines where his comrades just now were preparing to unleash a cloud of death in his direction. The Allied generals did not believe it would work, he had told them and now they put him opposite the German lines from which he had deserted.

Even despite his language problem he was able to get a pen and paper. He wrote a letter to his mother and tried to explain why he had deserted. That he believed that chemical warfare was to be banned and that he would now die for his belief. He went back watching the German lines, when suddenly a yellow cloud emerged from the trenches.

Historical Note

At exactly 18.00, on April 22nd 1915, the French and British soldiers at the front line of Ypern saw a yellow-brown cloud emerge from the trenches of the Germans. The first gas attack in the history of warfare had started. It is unclear how many soldiers died. Some sources say there were 5,000 dead and 10,000 wounded, others report 1,200 dead and 7,200 wounded.

However, from a military point of view, the attack was a failure. Even though the gas attack itself happened as planned, the Germans had not enough reserves to use the gap in the enemy front line because the generals had not believed the attack would be a success.

The Allied Forces did not believe in a threat from gas and therefore ignored all signs that the Germans were planning to attack. Observer planes, agents and even a deserter told them about the planned attack, but all were ignored. August Jaeger existed and truly deserted from the German 234 Reserve Infantry Regiment at the front of Ypern, however, he was not put to arms on the Allied side of Ypern and did not die from the gas attack of the Germans. Also, his motives to desert were not the preparation of the gas attack. He survived the war and was put in prison for treason 10 years after the war had ended.

After the war had gone stalemate, the Germans were looking for a way to break the enemy front line. The chemist Fritz Haber advised the use of chlorine gas that was stored in the tanks of the German chemistry industry as waste. He got the job and started to prepare a cloud attack from the German trenches. In the weeks of work, he let 1,600 big and 4,130 small steel tanks be filled with liquid chlorine gas and be dug into the ground.

Today, Ypern lives with the past. Wherever you look, there are cemeteries. The Allied Forces lost 200,000 men in the region of Ypern alone, 97,000 of whom are still where they fell. Today they are buried beneath a metre of mud. Every day three army trucks make their round to get the ammunition that the farmers just put on the side of the next street. These are brought to the barracks, where 10 boxes of ammunition are brought to explosion every day. That is still not enough; 28,000 more boxes are waiting to be neutralised, many of them still filled with dangerous gas. In 1917, every third grenade was a gas grenade.

Edgar Haener (15)
Institut Montana, Switzerland

Anticipation

Suddenly the short stretch appears a mile long. The red track glows like the red sand in the desert of Central Australia, the sun gleams down as if to mock my pathetic attempts to remain calm. Although I know perfectly well that there is a noisy crowd of both ally and predator, in my head everything is mute.

'On your marks!'

As I kneel there the sun continues to torment me and I begin to feel like the sun is laughing from one angle and the track, whose distinct rubbery smell fills my nostrils, from the other.

'Get set …'

As I lift my feet, which now feel like they are made of solid lead, into the start blocks, as the sun continues its attempt to burn every living creature. The track I have run so many laps on no longer has anything familiar about, it is now the coarse path that will either bring me to the water, will make me prey of the eagles circling above.

Bang!

As I run across that red track, all I hear is the sound of the great paws of the lions running very close to me. The eagles dive lower, but the gazelles in front are suddenly slower.

I fail to realise that I have run what seems endless, only about 10 metres after that desired line do my feet finally stop.

I have reached the oasis, the isolation is broken and I begin to hear the cheers from the crowd.

Sabrina Bleuler (17)
Instiut Montana, Switzerland

Fame Has Its Price

Once upon a time there was a robot, whose name was Mr PC. His biggest problem was that a robot couldn't become famous - which had been his dream ever since he had been switched on for the first time. Though PC used every possibility to find his way to fame, nothing changed. He didn't have his own perfect voice, so he couldn't sing. He wasn't smarter than other robots, and he couldn't write anything original. There just wasn't anything special about Mr PC. Most likely because robots are usually programmed the same way.

Life was passing him by, until one night, when sitting on his master's porch, he felt something he'd never felt before. It was a thunderbolt. Life suddenly switched. He could predict the future. He couldn't understand how, but he just felt the answer to any question pertaining to future events. Resurrecting his dreams of fame, he ran away from his master, heading to the closest newspaper.

The next day at 7am when his fellow citizens opened their morning newspapers, he became famous. At 10.32am he was already dead (if a robot can be called dead). His main processor had been destroyed in the experiments with the help of which scientists wanted to find the way to seeing the future.

This robot had been smart enough to understand the outcome of his visit to the newspaper. But it was his only shot at fame. Fame was with him with 3 hours and 32 minutes. Is such a short period of fame worth a life?

Olexander Karpenko (17)
Institut Montana, Switzerland

Perfection

As I close my eyes, I smell the smoke which blows in my direction. The fire is keeping me warm and I take another short glimpse of the thousands of beautiful stars above me. In the silence only the fire and the waves of the ocean can be heard. There is complete harmony between the four elements. The rays of the early morning sun awake me; the fire has turned into a pile of black, steaming coal.

I get up and walk in the direction of the ocean. The sand is still cold and a few birds can be heard, singing in the distance. The small waves tickle my stomach as I walk through the water. The beach is already quite some distance away and yet the water is not deep. Every grain of sand and shell can be seen underneath the water's surface. A few colourful fishes swim close to me. There is no one else, only nature and I.

I look in front of me. I can see how the ocean and the sky become one. This phenomenon of unity, also called horizon, the unity of two powers, wind and water is so amazing that I cannot take my eyes off it. I hark but there is complete silence, no cars, no children screaming. There is only the beauty and perfection of nature surrounding me. A perfection which is only found in nature and will never be replaceable by a human creation.

Marline Kipper (17)
Institut Montana, Switzerland

The Homecoming

Only at home could I feel safe and breathe freely. Coming back home was one of the best things about boarding school. It wasn't just the people and the places that I missed. Most of all I longed to regain that feeling of security, universal love and warm comfort of my childhood that I had lost when I left to study in a foreign country.

Today was different: I was coming home two weeks earlier than expected. My father had had a heart attack. My mother told me he would be alright and my presence was needed to lift his spirits. As the airplane touched the ground I felt like rushing out on the runway, reaching my parents, hugging them tightly and never letting go so that nothing would ever be able to hurt them again.

I immediately spotted my mother in the arrival area. A black scarf covered her hair, her eyes were red with crying. Her telling me, 'Father is not here anymore', was unnecessary, I was at once blinded by the realisation. I went absolutely numb - I did not know such painful emptiness was possible: no thoughts, no emotions. 'Cry, honey, cry!' was what Mother was urging me. The feeling of unreality was so strong, the grief and the tears had not yet arrived. I saw it incredibly sharp - my perfect, happy world was crumbling in front of my eyes. I suddenly remembered the piercing wind on the airport runway and understood: I would never feel safe again.

Krystyna Liakh (17)
Institut Montana, Switzerland

Untitled

Jonathan always found life mundane. Going through every day was a mechanical task and every day was homogeneous and plain. This thought permeated him since he was small, and from there became an adolescent, and from there a respectable young adult working a respectable office job. Boredom in his life was so much that he could hardly, at the end of the day, remember what he had done. However, when those rare moments of dramatic events came along, those short bursts of turmoil, emotion or simply adrenaline, he felt exhilarated by them.

In movies when disasters happen, such as plane crashes, hostage takeovers, world shattering natural disasters ... he always imagined himself being in that kind of situation. An erupting volcano in the middle of the city, tornadoes, a sudden rapid ice age ... all sensationalised every nerve in Jonathan's body. Because that is when the world has been turned upside down. That is when the order and structure of life twists into an iridescent chaos, and Jonathan struggling to go through it, not only surviving it, but dominating it, rising through it, to lead other people through tragedy, to forge a new path through a wrecked world. Heroism and glory, in an age wrought with greed and sin, seemed like an ecstasy-like miracle drug that saved him from the suffocating dullness.

These were his fantasies. These, were his calling. And on a September morning, he had his chance. A plane had flown into the building complex that sent a thunderous shock ...

Westley Tsou (16)
Institut Montana, Switzerland

The Birds Of Pleasure

They staggered to the Transit Motel, as they had numerous times before, convinced that this night would be the same as all the other occasions when they had entertained themselves with one or two of the birds of pleasure who lived and worked at the Transit Motel.

The four men entered the establishment as boisterously as ever, proclaiming to each other how their friendship was like an eternal flame that could only be extinguished through death. But the tone of their conversation quickly changed to one of business, reminded of their purpose by the pungent smell of jezebel juice and all the men that had passed through that same night. The four took their seats as they always had in the back corner of the room.

They were quickly joined by four birds of pleasure. Jérôme had always been the unlucky one of them all, always finding himself with the least exotic or charming of the birds. And pondering on himself why this always happened, she began to play with his palm as if it had all the secrets and all the troubles written on it throughout his life. Suddenly to tell Jérôme de st Amour that a great tragedy awaited him if he was to leave the motel that very night, and hoping not to obtain the words that she knew would come, those fabled words, 'Lads, let's go.'

As the four walked out led by Jérôme de st Amour, followed by her screaming and crying in the vain effort to convince him that what she had said was the truth up until the door where she was restrained by the Madame of the establishment.

The bird attempted to explain to the Madame what she had seen in his palm, only to be interrupted in mid-sentence by the noise of a carriage and screams.

She realised that there was nothing more that she could do because those screams were only of three of the four men who had entered the Transit Motel on that frightful night.

Wandile Mzikababa Mngomezulu (18)
Institut Montana, Switzerland

Science And Scientists

Science, how can we explain that word? Study of all aspects of human life, but maybe there is something more than that: search for answers, explanations or sometimes the need to know more things.

My story is based on this belief. It was exactly in 1952, I was 6 years old, when my doctor discovered a tumour in the upper part of my intestine. My parents could fortunately afford an operation, but there was not much knowledge about those peculiar tumours and how to proceed. As far as I can remember, I was extremely frightened but Mum and Dad were always by my side.

The operation finished successfully, but we had to wait until the results were ready. Two or three weeks of pain were over when the doctor told us everything was OK.

Hard times had finished finally, or they seemed to. In 1956, near my 10th birthday the tumour was back. At that moment, there were very few cases of a returning tumour so there was no information about it.

I had to put up with treatments and people that only told me what I wanted to hear.

After visiting six or seven doctors we decided to do what all of them told us. The only escape, another surgery. Nothing was for sure, there were possibilities of something happening but I couldn't surrender.

When the day came, I was really hysterical. When I entered the surgery room, they put me to sleep. I remember this moment as if it was now.

It felt so real, I was walking, standing in clouds. Somebody came towards me, without talking we spoke. Why did I want to return to life he asked? I answered: for my family. When I said that the sky fell and then I realised I was alive.

Sofía Posada (13)
Ivy Thomas Memorial School, Uruguay

Mother's Day

It was a rainy morning, Alan was just waking up at quarter to ten, because it was Sunday and fortunately he didn't have to work. It was Mother's Day, and his relationship with his wasn't quite a good one, so he was determined not even to give her a phone call. He prepared breakfast and then went for a walk along the beach as he always did.

While he was walking, he saw a young girl sitting alone sobbing. He stared at her for some time but she wouldn't realise, so after some minutes he asked her what was wrong. She replied, crying, 'I want to buy some white roses for my mother, but they cost three dollars and I'm afraid I have only one.'

'Come with me,' Alan suggested, 'I'll buy you the roses.' And with a big smile he took the girl by the hand to the flower shop.

The expression on the girl's face suddenly changed, and they both walked towards the nearest flower shop. When they reached the place, Alan bought the flowers and he even doubted whether to buy some for his mother or not, but finally he didn't. As they were leaving, he offered the girl a ride home, and she said happily, 'Oh yes! You can take me to my mother's!'

She directed him to the cemetery, where she placed the roses on a freshly dug grave. Alan returned to the flower shop and bought a bouquet for his mother.

Agustina Cordone (13)
Ivy Thomas Memorial School, Uruguay

Retirement Day

On the verge of retirement, Miles Ferguson had been working all evening on the murder case for which the trial began today, his *last* trial. His client, the defendant, a filthy, lying, little rich blonde who paid Miles enough money a day to cover his golf club's membership, plus some various taxes, had to become his main concern for the next few hours.

Thus, he chanted silently to himself while walking hurriedly through the cold corridors of the Los Angeles Judicial Department, *she's innocent, innocent*. He, of course, knew the multimillionaire heiress was guilty from the very start, but he had got an entire jury to start convincing of the opposite in just a few minutes.

Helena Petersen Lloyd was being accused of committing murder on her twenty-eight year-old boyfriend, who was about twenty years younger than her, on the afternoon of April 14th. Apparently, Helena had pushed the victim over her Beverly Hills mansion's second floor veranda into the open air during a domestic fight, making him fall over the living room's majestic chandelier and crash it to pieces over his own body. The media had described the scene as being 'revolting' and after paying a visit to the luxurious manor, Miles couldn't agree more.

While turning round a corner, Miles started thinking about the freedom of retirement, and promised himself he would go along with his wife, Kate, on one of those fancy cruises she so badly longed to take.

He stepped into court that day feeling freedom at its climax, a smile almost protruding from the usual sombre expression on his face. He was ready. This case was already his.

Juan Pablo Rossolino (14)
Ivy Thomas Memorial School, Uruguay

The Black Rider

Once upon a time in the Wild West, a strange figure appeared through the shadows. Riding a dark-coloured horse, he disappeared behind some trees. He and his stud were known as 'The Black Rider'.

The image I got of him was that he wore a big flat hat, black boots and a huge cloak that flew with the wind. I also saw a mask and I noticed he had a good saddle. Every single garment he wore was black. However, his horse was not really black although he looked it.

Monday 26th June, a very cold morning surrounded me while I heated some water for my tea. Every single day I knew what I'd done the day before, except during the night. After a good tea, I got ready to have a shower. I noticed some black clothes that appeared every morning in the bathroom, but I never knew where they came from. It was freezing so I got into the bath tub.

Minutes later I was all dressed up and ready to go out. I looked out of the window to see what the weather was like and saw a dark brown horse trailing around my garden. I mounted it and went for a ride.

Every morning it was the same routine, and I could never remember the night before. But I always had the same dream about an evening hero dressed in black …

Juan José De Feo (14)
Ivy Thomas Memorial School, Uruguay

That Game

It was a cold, dark night and I was at my grandmother's house just like every Christmas. I was in the backyard with my cousins and we didn't know what to do. We were twelve children, thinking of what we could do to have fun.

An hour later my cousin James said we could play a game called 'smee'. I refused to play that game, so all my cousins asked me what it consisted of and I began to explain. 'Smee consists of putting twelve papers in a bowl, one of which says 'smee'. We all sit in the living room and pick up the papers. When we all read the papers we put out the lights and the one who took the 'smee' must hide somewhere in the house.'

I finished telling them about the game and all my cousins were very excited with the idea of playing. I had already played this game before and something awful had happened. 'Can I tell you?' I asked my cousins.

'Well I was at a friend's house with ten more friends and the house was enormous. My friend Paul began telling me a story of a girl who had died in that house twenty years before. I felt very scared, but as there was a girl I had a crush on I tried to be brave. As we were very bored, we started playing 'smee'.

We all agreed to play. Fifteen minutes later we all went to find the 'smee'. When you are 'smee' and someone finds you, you have to be quiet, but if you're not 'smee' you have to say the word and keep looking. I found a girl and said 'smee' but heard no answer. I sat down with her, hoping she was the one I had a crush on. Minutes later my friend Sarah appeared and we started talking to the girl, but she didn't say a word.

Half an hour passed and nobody came so we went to the living room where the light was on. They were all there, and we had been sitting with a dead girl all the time. That's the end of the story,' I said to my cousins.

After I finished, they all wanted to go upstairs with their parents. Of course, we didn't play 'smee'.

Florenciq Gimene (14)
Ivy Thomas Memorial School, Uruguay

A Day In The Life Of …

Darkness. I lie safe in the smell of my brothers and sisters; woody, waxy, slightly stale. This is the still time, the time of waiting.

A sudden jolt and I'm heaved through the air with a wrench. I leave my stomach behind.

Jiggety, jiggerty, jog. Every day I'm shaken to the bone, then as suddenly as it started I'm thumped into place.

Gradually the light of day is opened up to me. My life is monochrome. I can't say it's a wonderful thing to be scraped, dragged, chewed and shaved intermittently throughout the day. See how I'm dragged across the surface, curled and flicked, leaving my trail of evidence. It's wearing me out to put it bluntly.

A panic moment. I feel I may be devoured. I'm being chewed and bitten, chewed and bitten. Stop, please stop!

Now it's frantic scraping and scratching. Round and round I go. I'm all over the place, I'm so dizzy. Just let me lie down. I've made my mark.

A moment's rest.

Whhheeeee!

That was magnificent I've just gone into flight. For a second or two I soared high in the air and then I was caught with a clap between two hands.

Shaving time. Oh the noise and the pain as I'm twisted, turned and ground against the blade. What is the point of all this?

The bell rings, I'm rapidly plunged into the darkness and the safe smell of my brothers and sisters.

Kirsty Keatch (13)
Morna International College, Ibiza

A Day In The Life Of A Lion Cub

'Time to get up,' said Mum.
    'OK, but it's still dark.'
    'But we have some meat for you,' said Mum.
    'But I like milk,' I said.
    'Come.'

'Mum wait … oh why do I have to have meat?'
    Meat, meat, meat, how I hate meat, I might go vegetarian - yes that's it! Now to find some good grass, I think there was some over there. Oh no, those funny, ugly things with big ears, a long nose and big, white, teeth-like things sticking out of their face! Oh well, I'll eat this grass … disgusting but it's better than meat!
    'Kids it's lunch,' said Mum.
    'What's for lunch?' I asked.
    'Meat!' Mum replied.
    'Oh no, I'm not eating that stuff!'
    'Well what else will you eat?' said Mum.
    'Grass,' I replied.
    Mum, who was now getting very angry, shouted, 'Grass … grass what are you, a vegetarian?'
    I butted in, 'Yes!'
    Mum, who looked like she was about to faint, said, 'You call yourself a man!'

Jack Walker (11)
Morna International College, Ibiza

Short Story

I jumped out of bed giving myself a head rush. It was twelve o'clock and Guila, my best friend, was arriving in just over half an hour. Tonight was going to be the best! It just kept going round and round my head. *Will I get in? Will I pass for an eighteen-year-old?* My eyes were wide open as I heard a noisy 4x4 arrive on my grey, pebbled porch so I anxiously slid down my spiral staircase.

'Guila!' I screamed with excitement.

We had a cold, juicy salad lunch in the lounge downstairs with my mum and my annoying sister.

'Come on let's go and see that fit new skirt I got!'

After about five intense hours of deep pampering and difficult dress wearing decisions we were ready to rock. We were going to Es Paradis, a club and we were going to get in like any eighteen-year-old.

'Sophie!' Maxi called. Maxi was my boyfriend and he had come to take us to the club.

'Cool babe, how are you?'

'Fine, ha! Ha! Let's go!'

Once at the door of the club shivers were running through my veins, butterflies in my stomach. I was so scared yet so excited at the same time. The doorman looked scary.

Yes! Yes! Yes! I got in! I officially looked like an eighteen-year-old! Oh how cool is that? Well, I'm gonna dance all night until I can't dance no more. Well, I'm in and that has made me the happiest person there is!

Sophie Lonsdale Ross (13)
Morna International College, Ibiza

A Day In The Life Of A Newborn Foal

Yawn! Oh another fresh day to wake up. *Yawn!* Wow! Wow! Look at that bright, colourful sun. The grass is freshly green and damp, it's so fresh it's waiting for me to eat it. I struggle to get up, I stretch my fluffy neck, to eat my early breakfast.

I haven't seen my mother yet! I panic, I run in small circles and then I shout, 'Mummy!'

My mother turns around and looks at me and says, 'Don't panic darling, I'm right here.'

I gallop up towards her and sigh. Every morning I thank God for such a beautiful life!

My lips are drying up, I need a drink, I lift my head up and stretch it to drink my mother's milk. It's cold and fresh, I love my mother's milk, it's also sweet. It's my favourite drink ever.

After my breakfast I want to have a run with my mum. I beg and beg, finally I get her to come. We run around, my mum goes twice as fast as me. After a while my legs are starting to ache, they're so skinny they can't carry me anymore!

I tell my mummy, so we head back home! *This is so much fun,* I say to myself. Finally we're approaching our own field. I have never run so fast in my life! The cold wind quickly crawls though my mane and short tail. The wind rushes past my face, it's an exquisite feeling, the wind slows down as we fall into a fast trot, which slows down into a walk.

Awww! I am exhausted with running, my legs tremble and my nostrils grow bigger and bigger, at the time. I slowly lie down because my legs are too tired to keep me standing. After a while I roll on the cold, fresh grass. My sweat turns hard and salty, so I want to take a bath. So me and Mummy jump in the lake across the field, *splash! Splash!* we're mucking about in the water.

'Yay!' I say.

'Neigh! Neigh!' Mummy says!

I'm soaking wet now and it's getting a bit chilly! I yawn and my eyes are getting tired.

Mummy says, 'Ooohh baby, you're getting tired, let's dry off and go to bed!'

I reply, 'That sounds like a good idea Mummy!'

We get out of the lake and shake the water off.

We slowly walk back to the herd, while we slowly dry off. As we arrive there, I collapse to the floor and fall into a deep sleep. My mummy lies her warm body next to mine, and falls asleep too. Today was a great day, but tomorrow will be greater and the next day will be the greatest! I hope!

Yawn! Yawn! Another morning to get up and enjoy life!

Dara Dorsman (12)
Morna International College, Ibiza

A Day In The Life Of Patch

Ouch! Get off! That tickles! Hey cut it out!

Mum was licking me again, I hate it, it tickles.

I stretch, get up and jump on my brother, I love play fighting, 'specially with my little sister, but she's not here today, Dolly must be playing with her. I win against my brother, (I always do), so I walk over to my water bowl, I'm always so thirsty in the mornings.

My big sister comes over and pushes me into it!

Hey!

I shake and go back to bed, I need as much sleep as I can get because Dolly is taking us to the Hippodrome soon where she will try to give us away. If I get given away I hope I go with my little sister or even better my mother but I know Dolly's mother wants to keep her.

Here comes Dolly with her mother and my little sister, this means we'll be going now.

Dolly picks me up and puts us in the car boot.

Her mother dumps my big sister on top of me and my mother pulls her off. At last we get there, Dolly pulls my little sister and I out and carries us around.

Behind us I can hear Dolly's mother asking a man if he wants my big sister. He says he already has lots of dogs, but then his wife comes along and says that one more dog won't make any difference.

Then she sees my brother and says she'll take them both.

No one will take my little sister or me, so Dolly's mum says we can stay with them.

I got exactly what I wanted and more.

Dolly Unsworth (12)
Morna International College, Ibiza

A Day In The Life Of A Relaxed Tiger

Here I am relaxing in my mate's kingdom enjoying the sun through my orange fur and my cubs learning how to hunt in the green grass instead of enjoying me for milk. It is all silent, the trees are not thrashing and there is no one entering my beautiful property and no prey eating my green grass.

I relax and smell the meat that my mate is bringing back for me a mile away. Who would enjoy my life more than me? While I am lying down I can feel how soft the ground is, touching my fur very softly. While my cubs come greeting Daddy back home and talking about his extraordinary adventure he drops the fresh meat beside me to enjoy like he's my slave.

He takes a rest beside me and we cuddle up like a fur ball, we get up and eat our amazing chunk of meat which is really all for me.

While we are eating our children run off and we have our own little private time alone at last, who could have a better life than me?

Sofia Schwarzkopf (11)
Morna International College, Ibiza

A Day In The Life Of A Ginger Kitten

Hi everybody, my name is Jackington, and I am 1 month and 9 days old. I have very dainty paws and a long tail.

My ideal day is waking up in my basket, well practically a king-sized bed, it is very snug. I curl up next to my fish-shaped cushion on the silk blanket. Then I have a drink and a bath in my tub.

After my soothing, warm bath it's time for breakfast, full English.

When I'm finished I scuttle down to the farm, my friend, well bestest friend, Gordon lives there. He pulls the limousine carriage.

When he pulls the carriage I jump on his head and snuggle into his mane.

When we get to the mansion, the coolest place ever, me and Gordon play for hours. The house alone is 17,000m² and it has 120,000,000m² of land.

Me and Gordon spend hours playing in the long green grass, blowing swiftly in the wind.

At 5 o'clock every day we go to the market, if it wasn't for Gordon I'd have a downright boring time.

After we've looked around the market, they usually take me to the groomers. My fur and paws get so messy after I've been to the mansion and the market, but I hate my groomers, all they do is tug at your fur and cause you pain.

Now it's 7 o'clock and it's dark, we go back to the house. By now I'm normally dirty again anyway.

When we get there they feed me this horrible stuff. I can just make out what it says on the box. 'Ca-t fud!' But then I get water, it's so refreshing after the whole day running round the garden in the mansion and the market.

Anyway, bedtime now, but my owner Nodrog lets me read my cat book about fairy tales, I love it.

This is probably my favourite thing in the day apart from playing with Gordon.

Then I fall asleep looking at the stars and the moon, they're as bright as ever. Nighty-night.

Oliver Tucker (11)
Morna International College, Ibiza

McCloud's Discovery

It was only 5am and a beautiful morning already. Only the chirping birds could be heard in the valley of Faresville. It was a small valley, with a river passing through the village. Today the river was calmer than normal, so it was even more quiet.

Mr McCloud was on his daily walk down the dusty roads of the sleeping village. This was the only time he left the house. McCloud had no friends and all his family had died a long time ago. He was a very lonely and mysterious man, a retired archaeologist, and a practical man: a scientist who believed in fact with no exception.

This walk he wanted to go take a look at the archaeology dig which was said to be haunted. Of course McCloud didn't believe such things. When he reached his destination, and was only a few centimetres away from the dig, he slipped and fell into the empty darkness of that deep hole.

He landed against a dark, rocky surface, and when he opened his eyes he saw something that his mind refused to believe: there seemed to be loads of dragons staring down at him, eyes wide open. Poor Mr McCloud was terrified but also astounded. He was completely frozen with fear. He couldn't even breathe. After a few minutes, which for him seemed like decades, he gathered the strength to get up. The dragons were still staring at him.

What he saw when he got up was amazing: a whole civilisation. A dome full of holes, humongous holes, with dragons coming in and out of them. The strange thing was the fact that none of the dragons had wings, although they could leap incredibly high. Everything was made of rock. In the middle was a huge statue of a dragon with wings.

The biggest dragon pushed his way to the front and breathed fire on McCloud. All McCloud saw was a stream of blue fire and then he felt completely different, he felt a lot younger, he looked at himself and saw *he* was a *dragon*. He was flabbergasted. After a few months to settle in he finally had found happiness.

McCloud was so happy in his new world, it was like starting his life from scratch. He played all day without a worry in the world. He had completely forgotten the old world. He knew that nothing would ever change because he knew that dragons lived forever. He was a happy dragon.

Jackson Braghieri (12)
Morna International College, Ibiza

Teenagers Go On The Rampage

New school rules passed this week has seen teenagers at the local school in uproar. The protest was quiet to start with, but built up into a frenzy of violence and book burnings, that had teachers running for safety in the staff quarters. Youthful violence spilled onto the streets, and neighbours were imprisoned in their homes, through sheer terror.

We had a little interview with one of the teachers we found hiding under the table. 'I am so frightened, all these kids trying to attack me and my staff, I don't know what has come over them,' said Mrs Camble.

We then had another interview with one of the rebellious kids. 'I despise this school, last year we were allowed to wear what we wanted and the rules were fewer and simpler'.

The police were brought in to the school to control the situation, once order was maintained the damage of the aftermath could be seen, the school cafeteria was burned down and graffiti was all over the bathroom walls and classrooms.

The ringleaders were brought in for questioning yesterday and further news will be covered tomorrow.

Ambra Peci-Malek (13)
Morna International College, Ibiza

A Day In The Life Of Anita Tinkle

Strangely enough, Anita Tinkle was a boy. He had extreme bladder conditions.

Anita woke up one day; just like any other, in his stained, wet bed. Anita stood up and went to brush his teeth and get ready for school. Once he put on his shoes he trickled down the stairs and into the kitchen.

'Hi IP Freely.'

'Oh, hi son how did you sleep?'

'Just as usual Ma, I wet the bed again.'

'Not again Tinkle, that's the sixth time in three days!'

IP Freely was Anita Tinkle's stepmum, she adopted him after hearing that his real parents, Mr and Mrs Peealot died from getting sucked into the toilet and drowned in their urine.

'Well Ma, I gotta flush to school!'

'OK son, don't forget your shoes!'

'Uhh … OK, Ma, smell ya later!'

Anita made his way to the door, and as he went out the door he met up with his two German friends, Ivana and Tinkle.

'Hey guys, how's it flowing?'

'Oh it's going vell.'

The three unhygienic friends made their way out the front gate and onto the main road.

'Anita Tinkle, Anita darling, are you wearing your diaper?'

Everyone around them laughed hysterically, even the two old people on the other side of the road, called Mr and Mrs Eve Hill.

'Uh!' Anita Tinkle blushed. 'No Ma, but don't worry!'

'No! No! I'll have Peter Panze bring some to school.'

Oh God, thought Anita to himself, *this is the most embarrassing day of my life!*

Although in actual fact it was just another day in the life of Anita Tinkle!

Joshua Rice (13)
Morna International College, Ibiza

Aljin's Riddle

An old man named Aljin showed the king a ruby he acquired during his travels one day, and the king immediately asked the traveller what he wanted in return for it. Aljin explained that the ruby was not for sale, but the king could have it if he could solve a riddle; however, if the king didn't solve it in three days, Aljin would get his crown. The king's son warned his father not to risk everything for a ruby, but the king couldn't help himself.

By the end of the third day, no one in the kingdom had managed to solve the riddle, so the king began to hand over his crown. Suddenly, however, a little girl in the back of the room called out. The king was so desperate by then that he allowed her to try and solve the riddle, and so Aljin repeated it for the hundredth time: 'Three men were walking one moonless night in total darkness. One man trips over a rock and the other hits a tree, but the last man walks all the way home in pitch-black darkness. How did he do it safely?'

The girl replied, 'The darkness didn't affect him because he was blind, just like I am.' And with that, Aljin was booted out of the kingdom and the little blind girl was rewarded greatly. The king, however, got his ruby and learned his lesson. So basically everyone lived happily ever after.

Atika al-Barwani (15)
Muscat Private School, Sultanate of Oman

An Unforgettable Christmas

'Hello … I'm fine … I'll be there. Who wants to spend Christmas alone anyway? … OK, Bye.'

'Can't you go faster?' I asked the taxi driver.

   'Sorry Sir, it's too foggy. I might have an accident.'

   'Never mind, I'll get off here,' I said, looking outside the window. All I could see was the bridge we were on.

   As I opened the door, I felt the bitterness in the air. I stepped out of the taxi and slammed its door angrily.

   I had a warm house which I could've spent Christmas in, I thought, *instead I decided to share the holiday spirit with my friends. Look where I am now!*

   The fog was getting thicker so that I could barely see my feet.

   'Do you want any help Sir?' said a voice behind me.

   When I turned around I saw a young boy leaning on his motorbike.

   'No,' I said, turning my back to him again.

   'I can help you get around the city,' he said confidently.

   I didn't want to waste anymore time, so I gave him the address and rode behind him on the motorbike. When he drove off, I couldn't see what was ahead of us.

After some time the young boy said, 'Here we are Sir.'

   I got off the motorbike and to my amazement I was standing in front of the right house!

   'How did you do that?' I asked in astonishment.

   'I'm blind,' he answered. 'It makes no difference to me whether the city is foggy or not,' he continued explaining.

Elias Khattar (15)
Muscat Private School, Sultanate of Oman

A Day In The Life Of A Lazy, Rich Man

Slowly the light peeped over the horizon. The morning was one of the sort that made one remember a trip to the Arctic, chilling and yet with an incredible blue sky.

The tranquil morning's silence was broken by a loud clanging of the opulent man's alarm clock. He snorted atrociously and picked up the reverberating alarm clock. With amazing strength for someone who has just woken up, he threw it into his bathroom. The noise stopped.

Unfortunately, for the not so dormant lump in the bed, a smart man-servant walked in - and if he didn't wake the lump, the smell of freshly baked cake definitely did!

Mr Gregor sat up and took three slices of cake. The man-servant left the room with the alarm clock. Once again it had to be repaired.

Meanwhile, Mr Gregor ignored the beautiful day outside and went into his ensuite bathroom to wash himself.

Mr Gregor never had breakfast. He went straight to lunch. After all, it was half-noon when he eventually rose.

After his luncheon (as he called it), he had his afternoon nap. Although his nap usually lasted two hours and twenty-five minutes, today it only lasted two hours and twenty-two minutes, due to an upset turkey on a farm a mile and a half away.

Mr Gregor angrily called his man-servant. 'Wellman! I want that turkey for my dinner, as a price for waking me up two minutes and forty-six seconds early!'

Thirty seconds later, Mr Gregor extended his rotund arm and seized his plush, black telephone.

'Ground floor, sixth floor speaking, Wellman is expected in fifty seconds with my tea!'

Wellman arrived at his master's door to hear soft 'piggy' grunts and loud, grotesque snores penetrating the silence.

This is how Mr Gregor lived, with the exception of the turkey.

Louisa Harris (12)
Pembroke House, Kenya

Humanity

He wakes up sweaty and shouting. As he turns around he sees this woman that he knew but had never seen before.

'You represent all hate and despair, you represent humanity and you shall be judged,' she says.

'Who ... who are you?' he asks.

'I am the air, breeze and the sea, I am your mother.'

Next time he opens his eyes he is in the court. A deaf whale is the judge and the jury is made up of the ozone, a polluted river, a dissected frog, a monkey from a lab and some fish.

The first witness is the sun and he says, 'One morning, I saw an otter looking for its love. He found her dead. She had been murdered to dress a killer, the otter doesn't understand, why do they kill for skin if they have their own?'

The second witness is a burnt forest that declares, 'Under my branches once I saw what they call sport. With weapons - dogs, they follow, kill and tear to pieces poor animals. They don't do it for need anymore now, it's called pleasure.'

José Robles (15)
Pinewood School, Greece

Changes And Spells

Are you one of those people who fancy stories about cute little girls who lose themselves in enchanted forests looking for innocent white bunnies? Well I was, until the day I had to sleep in such a girl's house and that changed it all.

My name is Clementine and I live at 24th Street in Cross Avenue. Alice, my best friend, lives right next door to me. She has dark brown hair and her skin is as white as unwritten paper. There has always been something strange about my friend Alice who makes an effort to keep to herself. She would always refute my pleas for sleepovers until this one time.

That afternoon I was packing to go to the sleepover when, all of a sudden a loud scream pierced the air. It was coming from next door. A cold chill ran down my spine. I hurried, stuffing my pyjamas in my bag and tripped all over myself to get to Alice's house.

Immediately after I rang the bell Alice's mother appeared at the door as if she was hiding right behind it, ready to chase away whoever the scream had brought to her house. In a voice I could hardly make out, she explained that I could not spend the night with Alice and that I had to sleep in the guest room. Something in her tone of voice made me feel that there was no room for negotiation so I did exactly as I was told.

Some time later I was in deep sleep when another terrible scream broke the night and my dreams into a thousand pieces. It was coming from Alice's room. I had to find out what was happening. I got out of bed and started down the dark hall. All of a sudden Alice's door was flung open and I found myself face to face with a large, fierce, white bunny. For some reason and in all my fright I could still realise that the face looked very familiar. I tried to go towards it but I saw that its intentions were not good, so I started to run. It chased me all the way to my house.

When I was safely locked in, I told my mum just what had happened and to my surprise not only did she believe every word of my story but also she took me by the hand and explained everything. Apparently Alice was under a spell! A spell that turned her into a killer rabbit right after sunset! Alice was 12 years old at the time just as I was and that made me sympathise with all of her sudden changes in mood and all her outbursts, as I knew what it was all coming from. But this was just a bit too much. I never complained about the changes I was feeling in me again. Oh! And I never went anywhere near rabbits for the rest of my life!

Melissa Zagka (12)
Pinewood School, Greece

The Story Of Whirl And Twirl

Whirl and Twirl, two adorable squirrels, are sitting on a big oak tree in my great grandma's backyard in Robersonville, North Carolina, USA. It's a warm, sunny, late afternoon and they're resting on a large branch gazing at the sunset, remembering their childhood years.

On one such afternoon a long time ago they got separated from their mother while they were going to a concert to watch Britney the chipmunk singer. A group of chipmunks came between their mother and them. By the time they moved away their mother was nowhere to be found. That night Whirl and Twirl slept on a pile of leaves.

The next morning they found themselves sleeping in the hollow part of a tree and with six yellow eyes staring at them. Apparently, without realising it, they were carried there the night before, while they were asleep. There was a mother, a father and a baby racoon watching them carefully and waiting for the squirrels to wake up. The racoons treated them with kindness. They bathed and fed them and had them like their own children for a few days. Whirl and Twirl were happy with the racoon family but they knew that they had to leave to find their own mother and father.

One fine morning they set out to find their parents. After a day of searching they found a big oak tree. Whirl and Twirl had found their parents. They were so happy to be all together again. Unfortunately that same day the catcher from the animal shelter caught the whole family of squirrels and took them to the shelter.

At the animal shelter all of the animals were very kind and friendly. Whirl, Twirl, their mother and father were having a great time.

A week later a young girl called Susan came to the shelter with her parents to find a pet. She had two choices; Whirl and Twirl, so she took them both home. Once again Whirl and Twirl were separated from their parents.

Today they are still with Susan who is my great grandma. They live in Susan's backyard and will never leave her. Up until this very day they are the oldest squirrels in the world.

Tiffany-Maria Waddill (12)
Pinewood School, Greece

The Trojan Horse

Silence reigned among the soldiers and their leader Odysseus. The success of this mission depended on it. If the Trojans discovered that the gigantic wooden horse was a trap hiding fifty soldiers instead of a gift left by the Greeks, then the whole mission would be ruined. Stealth and precision were a necessity.

They sat patiently in silence. All were thinking of their ten years away from home and family, ten years of war, fighting to get the beautiful Helen back to her husband, King Menelaus. They thought of the past few days' events, how Odysseus, inspired by Poseidon, had the idea of the wooden horse, how they had used the wood from their ships to build it and how they had concealed themselves in it while the rest of the Greeks went and hid elsewhere. Finally they thought of how they would go home if the mission were successful. This helped them through the long hours of silence.

It had been a long day. The Trojans, discovering the wooden horse, brought it into the city. Then the celebrations began and lasted until midnight. Finally, when everybody was asleep, Odysseus and his men lowered themselves out and silently killed the guards. They then opened the main gate and signalled the hiding Greek army. The city of Troy was charged and destroyed, leaving no inhabitants alive. The war was finally ended and the beautiful Helen was returned to Menelaus.

Elias Tselentakis (16)
Pinewood School, Greece

Confinement

Darkness chokes my senses until I silently beg for release, though glaring lights assault the room I'm currently in. I know my fellow prisoners feel the invisible darkness, too. Their eyes, once bright and spirited, now advertise to the world that their owners have died inside. My kindred sit unmoving at their assigned positions, empty shells of what they once were. I shudder to think how I could ever end up like that. I try lifting my head to search for an indication of how much longer I would be here, but my fatigue has the better of me. I slump in defeat. It's hopeless.

Horror stories of this place that I'd half forgotten emerge from the furthest reaches of my psyche, reaching up from my endless plains of boredom and despair to grip me with icy claws and drag me down to some unspeakable place of merciless torment. I shake my head, rid myself of the perturbing visions and scold myself for letting my imagination get the better of me. If my friends were here, they'd keep me from going insane, but by now they've probably moved on with their lives and forgotten about rescuing me. I wonder if they remember me at all.

'Right you lot,' a stern voice breaks the silence.

Click.

Our warden stands by the now unlocked prison exit with a humourless smile on his otherwise dispassionate face. 'Your hour of after school detention is officially over,' he drones. 'You may go home.'

Diane Go (16)
Port Moresby International School, Papua New Guinea

Lost

Aurora, a strong confident officer of the elite Serpent Unit had for many years imagined living in a small town with her future husband Jack Slater. Her life could never have taken a more dangerous route, a route that would change her views of the world, her job and everything she ever knew.

Aurora had grown up in a rural area and she never felt as if she belonged anywhere, but while travelling by train to see her parents she noticed an advertisement for the police and how they would welcome any newcomers, Aurora's brother had been the victim of an unsolved crime, the police had done little. Now was the time to change it all.

After years of extensive training and determination she was accepted into the Serpent Unit who only dealt with extreme threats and only took on extreme people. The unit is funded through several great powers and after seventy years, the identities of these governments remain unknown.

While preparing for a mission Aurora received a phone call.

'I warn you not to go through with this.' The voice was masked. 'Those men have very 'useful' weaponry, let this go.' Even though he knew the faithful officer would not stand down, his position needed her to. 'You may think I'm joking, many people think that, but we need you to be alive so I can settle an agreement.' If this failed then his life would not be worth spit.

'One, I won't drop this lead and two you and your agreement can burn in Hell.' An empty threat.

'Does April twenty-fifth spark any memories, this April?' He knew it would, it was Aurora's wedding day …

Simon Williams (16)
St Andrew's International High School, Africa

Saint Andrew's ... Teachers Bored?

Strange things have been occurring at Saint Andrew's International High School since Friday 13th April. A student called Lola Zamgy noticed that all the teachers were acting in a rather odd fashion, late to class and rushing to leave at the end of the lesson. When she mentioned it to her classmates they just ridiculed her.

About a week later, various teachers began to disappear, including the headmaster and both the deputy heads.

The school had now become like a students' wonderland, with over half the teachers missing. No one knew why or where they had disappeared to and if they were coming back, until ... this Lola girl overheard two teachers talking about 'the one-way tickets' to 'the room'.

She did not mention anything to the others because she knew that they wouldn't believe her. She thought of the least likely place in the school for teachers to be ... and the tuck shop area came into mind. She made a plan to skip class and explore the tuck shop.

She was all alone. Suddenly she recognised the sound of the 'Beatles'. It couldn't be the sixth formers because they wouldn't be caught dead listening to them! She hesitated then carried on towards the sound of the music. As she got nearer, she smelt a strong scent of alcohol. The music led her to the door of the tuck shop.

Then, she heard a deep voice; it sounded like the maths teacher's voice, he said, 'Teaching was so boring but we don't ever have to go back!'

A huge uproar from the other teachers followed.

Lola was taken aback. But decided to open the door, she gently turned the handle, pushed the door open and there, in front of her very eyes ...

Kavita Savjani (13)
St Andrew's International High School, Africa

A Day In The Life Of A Soldier Going To War

The moon lay eclipsed behind dark clouds. As I slowly rambled off the peaceful beach and onto the lonely and dark road my heart sank, six months with Greg's awful 'fresh' home-style cooking and without family, I couldn't bear it. I sighed then walked down the road, my feet only stepping on the white, untouched road line.

After a mile, I automatically turned left as my mind had previously taken this route and gone through these emotions. The growling of unhealthy ship engines came into audible range when I entered the grey and gloomy surroundings that lurked about the harbour. When my worn out boots walked over the pale wood decking the thump of them accompanied another sound, the sound of water being whirled by spinning propeller blades.

I stepped onto the ship and into greater depression. The thought of being killed on my mission with the addition of not being able to see my family throbbed in my head.

I took a smile on board as I passed the captain. I wanted to show my manliness to him, he probably knew it was phoney though, because the moment my back was towards him my posture slumped (my smile died too). I kept my head hunched throughout the descent to my bunk. The bland, grey walls and floors matched the dull dockyard.

When I reached my bunk, I said a prayer then hoped for the best as I docked into an uncomfortable object, known as a bed.

Aum Dasani (14)
St Andrew's International High School, Africa

A Day In The Life Of A Cricketer

Ring, ring. The loud alarms vibrated on this early Sunday morning. I excitedly jumped out of my enormous bed and looked through the window at the cricket ground that I would be playing on in a few hours. I wore my Indian cricket kit, ate my nutritious breakfast and then I sped to the ground in my Mercedes-Benz.

'Hi Rahul,' the other team players said to me. We discussed the plan we were going to use to try and beat Australia. After that I went for the toss.

Twenty minutes later we were bowling to Australia's opening batsmen. Unfortunately they were smashing super sixes. We finally got a wicket with our famous spinner, Anil Kumble. Despite losing a few wickets Australia still managed to get three hundred runs.

After our delicious lunch it was our turn to bat. The team was playing well. The game became very close; we needed four runs off two balls. Brett Lee bowled a beautiful yorker. Sachin was bowled out. I walked onto the ground and got a standing ovation. Everybody was shouting, 'Rahul, Rahul.' I got into position to face my first ball. My heart was pounding rapidly. The fastest bowler in the world was bowling. My eyes were on the ball. My bat swiftly came down. I felt a smooth connection with the ball. I looked straight ahead; the ball was racing to the boundary. Everyone in the stadium ran onto the pitch. We'd won.

Rahul Kotecha (13)
St Andrew's International High School, Africa

The Orphan

I am Zikomo which means 'thank you' in my language; Chichewa and I are orphans. I'm 14 years old and I've been an orphan for 7 years. My life is a unique one but I'm free which makes it fun.

I wake up in the morning freezing cold every day and the bridge (I usually sleep under a bridge) has been invaded by ants because of the rainy season, so I now sleep in the park. At around nine I have breakfast; I go to a 'free restaurant' the bin.

McDonald's bins are the best but sometimes bigger guys get there before me. When I'm done I spend the rest of my time begging for money, sometimes the bins are empty so the money I get helps me with my lunch.

In the afternoon I hang out with my friends and we always have fun. Usually we like to play soccer and other games and this goes on till the evening until we start begging for money again.

I don't have a home so I have to find one. It is hard to find a warm place during the rainy season but I've found a secret alley which is well enough for the cold nights.

Every time I go to sleep I wish that I had parents but until my wish comes true tomorrow will be no different from today.

Tuto Kalitera (13)
St Andrew's International High School, Africa

A Day In The Life Of A Victorian Child

It was a dawn of another dreary and tiring day. The sun had just risen but instead of welcoming a new day, all I longed for was the nightfall where I could have my three to four hours of sleep.

I was destined to be born in 1855 when Queen Victoria was on the throne. It was also in my 'kismet' that I was born in a poor family where I was expected to earn my keep. I had barely learnt to speak but my parents were proud of me - not because I was an extremely beautiful toddler but I was an active child. My favourite hobby was sweeping the floor.

Hobby, became a passion and passion turned into obsession. I was encouraged by my parents because I was earning our 'daily bread'. It made me feel extremely important. I, Charles Edward Martin at five years, was feeding my parents rather than them feeding or looking after me.

I was, in this era of child labour and was readily employed by everyone because of my size, ease of submission and cheapness. Sweeping and cleaning windows were my daily routine that I was sure that I sometimes even made these hand actions in my sleep.

In a couple of years I would turn ten, then it would be impossible for me to work in a textile mill. What did the future hold for me? Was my dream of becoming a doctor ever going to come true? I doubted it.

I sometimes wondered what if I had been born in an affluent family, would my life be better or worse?

Sabah Zaveri (12)
St Andrew's International High School, Africa

A Day In The Life Of Prince Charles

Riiinng … the alarm clock rang aloud. I stretched out my arm to switch off the ring.

I turned and saw my wife Camilla still in peaceful stupor. She is not a morning person as was Diana, who was used to early starts with the kids. Come to think of it, Camilla has more handsome features unlike Diana who was positively a beauty.

Well, anyway, it's all fate. My marriage to Diana was only to pacify the people and my totally domineering mother. The love of my life has always been Camilla.

I feel rather lethargic this morning. I don't think that I will be walking the corgis around Balmoral today. I feel totally exhausted.

As I get out of bed I step straight on Harry's hiking shoes. Damn, why the hell can't he put his shoes where they belong?

I wash myself and get ready for breakfast which is usually served to me in my private quarters. Let's see what it'll be today. Suddenly I feel like mashed potatoes and baked beans.

I look for my diary as I wolf down my breakfast. I'm sure I left it on my bedside table last night. As I go to look for it, Camilla lies awake with her morning cup of Earl Grey tea. She's reading the paper and mentions another article on her looking like my mother. I ignore her and leave the room to finish my breakfast.

I look into my diary and look at my schedule. I have a lunch with my mother today, no doubt to talk about my reign to the throne. Mother wants to bypass me and give the crown to William. There are lots of meetings on today, and aah, the best part of the day - fox hunting with the boys.

I go back to my room and shower. Don't want to be late.

I pick out a nice silk suit, made by Armani. Diana loved to dress me and some of these suits are part of her collection.

I am only fashionably late for my first meeting. The morning runs smoothly. My mother even cancels the lunch so I go for a swim and have a short nap before the fox hunting with William and Harry.

The day finally comes to an end. I am exhausted and can't wait to go to bed.

Shaun Anadkat (12)
St Andrew's International High School, Africa

Killed For Love

It was October 1956. I had just met the lovely Fiona, it was love at first sight. We engaged in the normal first date shy conversation, but gradually built up courage as we went along. After the day was over and I was sure Fiona was safely home, I went to bed to dream about the day gone by.

'Philip, Philip,' shouted Dave.

I was at lunch with my best friend. I had been dreaming about Fiona. Of course, Dave wished to know why I was so out of this world, so I told him all about Fiona. Dave wasn't really the romantic type and he told me to forget about her, but I couldn't, I was deeply in love.

It was almost a week since Fiona and I had met. My desire for her had been building up over the past few days. It was like a fire burning inside of me. I had been walking in the market square when I saw her, my lovely Fiona. Our eyes met and an hour later I found myself in her bedroom. Suddenly she got up and closed the door. What happened in there was unmentionable by words.

August 1957. Raymond was born. Me and Fiona had to marry in haste due to the upcoming baby. Life went on well till one day, me and Fiona were on our way to see Raymond's aunt. We were walking on a busy road when some fool, who was overwhelmed with Fiona's beauty, lunged forward and gave her a smack on her behind. I got so mad I verbally attacked the other man. The anger in me was so great, burning up inside of me. I drew a dagger from my pocket and slit the other man's throat. He fell down and slowly bled to death. Of course, I knew I had entered a whole lot of trouble.

It had been two years since the incident. A day had not gone by that Fiona had not said what I did was not necessary. That night was another night that she had brought up the subject. I sat in silence and listened. We were in our new house that we had bought to raise our family. Fiona was once again expecting a baby, Raymond was now two, soon to be three. Suddenly the door broke down and a mob of men ran in, all with daggers.

One of them who seemed like the leader said, 'So you killed my friend. Well, now it's my turn and I will start with your lady friend here.' He spoke in a slow, threatening voice.

I rushed forward to fight and threw a blow at him. His friends, of course, rushed in to help and threw me off. Their leader then came forward and shot a few blows into me, while his friends tightly held me. He turned again to Fiona and threw her onto a chair. I tried to get

Young Writers – T.A.L.E.S. From Across The World

away, but the other guys held me tightly to the ground, not letting me escape. He took out his dagger and lifted it well above Fiona's bulging stomach. I knew what was to happen next, so with all my strength I got free and dived in front of Fiona, just as he let his hand fall. He stabbed me in the chest. After realising this they quickly ran out of the house. I gasped for breath while Fiona, my lovely wife, wept over me.

I took in my last breath and managed to gasp out, 'I love you,' then darkness engulfed me.

Yamikani Nyang'wa (12)
St Andrew's International High School, Africa

Hansel And Gretel

Once there were two children, brother and sister, who were very unlucky. First they had a perfectly horrible mother and weak, wimpish father. Second, there was a terrible famine in the land so that no one had enough to eat. And thirdly, the horrible mother said to her husband, 'We can't feed four mouths but we might still be able to feed two. Let's get rid of the kids.'

Their father was too weak and wimpish to say no.

Hansel and Gretel were dumped in the depths of a forest in the middle of winter and left to die - of cold and starvation. Tragic, eh? Imagine the poor children lying in the snow, holding each other tightly, waiting for death.

Forget it. Hansel and Gretel were made of sterner stuff. In spite of the bitter cold, they set off hand in hand through the forest, not after their parents - they'd had enough of them - but in the opposite direction, and before long they came upon a little cottage among the trees.

Hurrying near, they found that the cottage was made, not of bricks and mortar, but, would you believe it, of biscuits and cakes with windows of sugar.

They did not know that inside this cottage lived a sweet, old, white-haired, apple-cheeked lady who was actually a wicked witch.

She had the most horrible habit. She ate children. Hansel and Gretel, being terribly hungry, set about eating bits of the cottage.

Hansel had pulled off a piece of the roof and Gretel had smashed a window when out came the witch.

'Ha! Ha!' she cackled. 'You're just in time for my evening meal.'

'Oh good!' they said. 'We're starving. What's for supper?'

'You are,' said the witch. 'The oven's nice and hot, all ready for you.'

Hansel and Gretel looked at one another.

'I think she's a cannibal,' said Hansel.

'What's that?' asked Gretel.

'Someone who eats people.'

'Raw?'

'No, cooked.'

'Oh,' said Gretel. 'Why do cannibals eat people?'

'Because they're hungry.' Hansel looked admiringly at his little sister. 'Gretel,' he said, 'you aren't just a pretty face. Come on!'

Between them the children dragged the wicked witch inside and smeared her all over with lard, and shoved her in her own oven.

Later, when they'd eaten as much witch as they could manage, they put the rest out in the snow to keep, and polished off the cottage for afters.

Wasfeeya Altalib (11)
St Andrew's International High School, Africa

A Day In The Life Of A Goblin

I woke up one morning to find I was a … goblin. Yes a goblin, like the ones with long pointy ears and a serious face. I didn't know I was a goblin at the time so I walked downstairs for breakfast thinking everything was normal. I could smell the freshly cooked bacon and eggs. As I sat down my father removed the newspaper away from his face and said, 'Son, please pass …'

He looked at me for a while and then screamed. And I'm sure you know men don't normally scream so I must have been really ugly. My mum then turned around and said, 'What's wrong dear?'

She screamed when she looked at my face. I thought something must be wrong with me, so I looked in the hall mirror and screamed. I then sprinted out of the front door. My parents had their eyes fixed on me, looking horrified.

I asked myself how and why did this happen to me? And I was definitely not going to school looking like this! I decided to go to my favourite place, apart from home, and that is where the pond was. When I arrived I sat on a bench and gazed at the ducks. Time flew and I still just sat there. Then the sun started to set and I dozed off to sleep.

I woke up the next morning in my bed. I thought it was all a dream. I went downstairs to find … both my parents were ugly goblins. I thought, *oh no, not again!*

Mark Staples (12)
St Andrew's International High School, Africa

The Smelly Sisters

Once upon a time, in a faraway land called Nox, there lived two ugly sisters called Rule and Rula. Rule and Rula lived in a small house in the middle of the forest. One day the king announced that whoever rescued the prince would be his bride, so the two sisters set out on their quest to defeat the dragon and rescue the prince.

When they got to the dragon's cave they both shouted, 'Dragon, give us the prince or we'll huff and puff and blow this cave down.'

'Not on the hairs of my chinny-chin-chin,' he growled.

They huffed and puffed and blew the cave down. As the sisters entered the room the dragon was just about to cook the prince in a huge pot filled with boiling water when the sisters opened their mouths and let the dragon breathe in their rotten cheese and manure-smelling breath.

The dragon immediately turned yellow and fell to the ground with a big thump. The sisters quickly ran to the prince, eager to be his bride. The prince was horrified and told them that he did not want to marry either of them. Rule and Rula were heartbroken. They carried him back to their small house and imprisoned him in the cellar. They decided that if they couldn't have him, no one would.

Whitney Bartlett (12)
St Andrew's International High School, Africa

The Dragon's Lair

Two spirals of smoke came from within the dark entrance to the mysterious cave, the cave where the dragon dwelt. Not just any dragon, this one was colossal. He was not only big, but he possessed great cunning. This he used to draw unwary travellers into his mystic lair. In this way, many entered, and one came out alive. Using this method the dragon slowly devoured the people of the small village named Kligget, where people lived in constant fear of the merciless beast.

One day the grief-stricken people of Kligget decided that they had to try to put a stop to the killings. After an extremely long and serious council, they eventually decided to send the village's best fighter to challenge the dragon and then defeat him. The man, if he succeeded, he would be awarded the dragon's gold, a tidy sum; if the dragon had not devoured the hundreds of people's jewellery along with their flesh. The man that was chosen was called Kaggs, he was a tall, strong man with bulging muscles. Surely he could defeat the dragon?

Kaggs walked boldly into the dragon's lair and after three days the people of the village gave him up for dead. He was never seen again.

An ambitious boy aged 13 volunteered to fight the dragon. His father had been one of the many victims. The boy wished to avenge him. The council decided that he could go, but on the condition that if he died, they would not be to blame. So the boy set forth on his noble quest, he carried his sling and a sharp dagger. Going into the cave, he heard a low growl. Foolishly he slung a rock into the darkness. The dragon greeted him with a mighty roar that shook the ground. By now the boy, named Garth, was accustomed to the dark and witnessed his enemy before him. With a loud cry, he dived onto the dragon's scaly back and drove the dagger deep into the dragon's brain. The gold was his, the village was saved and his father was avenged.

Peter Harrison (12)
St Andrew's International High School, Africa

Outbursts From Townspeople As Bulldozers Tear Down Kamza Park!

Protestors gather around the fence of our famous game park Kamza Park. There are more than one hundred and fifty people clutching signs and banners of anger and disagreement. The manager says they will have to go soon as they are distracting his men from work but they don't look as if they are giving up as they stand gaping at the bulldozers tearing down the ancient gum trees.

It all began when Mr Holmes signed the contract which gave permission to build a huge new road right through the middle of the park.

Mr Holmes' (the owner of the game park) secretary, Mrs Matrian, says that she's amazed he would do such a thing and said, 'It's horrific'. But she is determined that Mr Holmes did not sign it. 'He loves his animals too much to do such a thing'.

Also a person, who does not wish to be named, has seen men, while out for a jog, walking on forbidden ground and carrying strange objects which looked to him like measuring instruments before Mr Holmes signed or even knew about the contract. Police are investigating further.

The animals in the park include eight lions, three cubs, more than two hundred monkeys, baboons, impala, different birds and buffalo (water).

A protestor says, 'These animals belong to freedom!'

Alison Soye (12)
St Andrew's International High School, Africa

A Day In The Life Of …

I can't bear it any longer. Really, I am sick and tired. This year started four months ago and it is the fourth time that I have to enter the operation room to be sewn. Do you really think that I can live with it? Imagine, every morning I have to walk more than 10 blocks carrying books, copybooks and a lot of silly things that are not useful at all. Can anyone tell me, do I deserve this? Does anybody take into account my age? I think that I am old enough. After 15 years of work, and after four different bosses, I believe, no, definitely I am sure that I need to get my pension. I am not asking for too much. I don't want anybody using me anymore, just once a week to go to rugby, but no more than that. Do you know what it is to be all the time on the floor with nobody paying attention to you? Thrown in the sidewalk, do you know what that means? It is not fair. Definitely it's not. I always go with him everywhere and take all his things. I spend more hours with him than anybody else. I know everything about him. I know that he smokes, and I don't tell his parents. I saw the package in the small front pocket. I am like a friend. Why does he continue treating me like that? I am always broken, on the floor, dirty. The only moment I am clean is when his mother cleans me. But one minute later I am dirty again. Why can't he love me as I love him? Because, after all, I appreciate him, he is my owner. Although he can have a new one, he chooses me. And I am thankful for that. So after all, I just want to know why he doesn't appreciate me as I appreciate him. I am totally tired and confused. The only thing that I want to know is why I wasn't meant to be a girl's schoolbag?

Agustina Martinez Llobet (17)
St Brendan's College, Buenos Aires

A Day In The Life Of A Fugitive

The trip back home was beginning. More than an hour separated him from the warmth of his house. This was the kind of night he hated. The twenty metres that separated the road where he got out of the taxi and the train station were enough for the heavy rain to wet his clothes. It was winter and night had arrived early. Waiting for the train to come, and inside his wet clothes, he could feel the pain the freezing wind produced on him. There was no one inside there. The drops crashing on the metallic roof and the wind screaming were the only sounds he could hear. The bad illumination made it impossible for him to finish reading the newspaper. His sight was focused in the darkness of the night. He was thinking in nothing when the hoot announcing the coming of the train froze his blood. The screeching doors violently opened. The dull yellow light let him see that he was alone in the wagon. He sat down next to a window and took the newspaper out. A calm whistle called his attention. It suddenly stopped. He turned round but noticed nothing strange.

Confused with the rain, he could distinguish a harmonic sound of steps. He heard them quite near him and he was about to look behind him when a heavy hand held his shoulder. 'Your ticket please?' He held his breath. Without looking at his eyes, he extended his shaking hand holding the ticket. 'Thank you …' His strong voice was vanished by a thunder clap. A deep silence then seized the situation. He had managed to escape unrecognised once again …

Agustín Dîaz Carvalho (17)
St Brendan's College, Buenos Aires

My Mind

It was a dark and rainy winter morning, rain formed bubbles on the floors of a huge castle that lay on the hills of an enormous farm. The inside of the castle was full of expensive decorations, columns brought by Colon to Argentina in 1942, enormous doors made of wood with copper-made doorknobs and lots of paintings by important Spanish painters who lived some centuries ago.

We were in front of a fireplace that was also surrounded by expensive mouldings. We were playing chess and after my opponent made some strange moves I felt something was going to happen. My mind, my whole head, was going through lots of thoughts. It went here and there trying to come to a conclusion about why he had made those moves. It was not common for him to play like this. He was definitely thinking about something else.

Perhaps he was just distracted by the rain that started making strange sounds on the roof. I went on playing without asking him what was wrong.

It was after an hour that I made the final move, the one that would end the game and turn my opponent crazy. He started throwing everything to the floor, even my 100-year-old paintings. That's the reason why, after making an attempt to stop him (I obviously couldn't because of his fury) I called Perkins for him to call the police.

To my relief, they came fast and stopped this animal in fury, who was seeking for things to be destroyed in front of me.

This was not a usual way of acting in him. He just turned crazy for a chess game. This was not the normal reaction of a Harvard student after playing a chess game and losing it against a world champion on the subject.

The day after this happened, I went to visit Fred Collins in the asylum. I asked him what had happened to him but he just didn't answer. The only thing he said was, 'Andy Lister, *you* are the next one.'

I was worried. I just wondered what was going to happen to me. His face was the only thing I could think of. It was disgusting.

But when I woke up the next morning I saw that everything was different. Anger, fury and a wish to destroy what I saw came to me. My mind was so disconnected from the outside world. It was definitely destroying *me*.

Gaston González Abad (16)
St Brendan's College, Buenos Aires

A Day In The Life Of Little Henry

Henry was a poor fourteen-year-old boy who worked cleaning the city. He always sent letters to the Queen because he wanted to talk with her about something that worried him, but she never received them.

One day Queen Victoria gave a speech in the park of the city. Henry and all his friends were there, listening to it. He thought that the Queen was going to talk about his letters, but he got very disappointed when the speech finished and she didn't talk about them. He ran after the Queen to ask her if she had received the letters, but the guards didn't let him see her.

Two months passed and nothing happened with the letters so he decided to go to Buckingham Palace to talk with the Queen. He managed to convince the guards outside to let him enter. When he approached the Queen's bedroom he knocked on the door and entered. The Queen was surprised about this, and she asked him, 'What's your name?'

He answered, 'M-m-my name is Henry, Your Majesty.'

The Queen and Henry talked for about three hours. Henry told her, 'I have to tell you something important.'

The Queen answered, 'Come on, tell me.'

'Well, I believe that all the children in this city deserve a happy childhood. I think that we should stop working in order to play, run or do whatever we want to do,' he answered.

Some days later the Queen had a meeting with her advisors and Henry. There, she announced that Henry was the new children advisor. Since that day children are very happy and can enjoy life, with Henry's help.

Sofia Ferandez Perotti (13)
St Brendan's College, Buenos Aires

The Honourable Soldier

I was on the way to the coast of Normandy. As the waves were splashing fiercely against our colossal disembarking launch the wind was humming gently on my ear. There were cries and prays on the ship of death. Some war mates were looking forward, expecting the worst.

As I looked at the black sky, the wind became freezing and stormy. I knew I was getting closer. The drop-bullets smashed into my face like stones falling from the air. When I turned round, I got astonished when I saw the biggest fleet I've ever seen before. My ship was like an ant in a formicary. As I faced forward, I thought a thunderstorm was approaching but I was wrong. A bomb from on high crashed into the ship next to ours. My helmet fell into the messy blue water.

The ship almost sunk, but I wanted to keep living. I strongly held my loaded Uzi and stayed calm. There were incandescent pieces of metal flying freely through the sky and crushing other ships. I slowly turned my head backwards. I saw bombs falling to my allies' ships, it was a mix of anger and fright. The awful sound of bombs going out from a cannon was like a thunderstorm that strikes in the same place, the boat.

Terrified, I turned my head forward and saw hundreds of German flags waving over the nearest hills. The ship stopped, opened its front gate, and my mates and I began to run on the wet sand as fast as possible.

I got shot in my chest, it was bleeding, but there was no pain. The Nazi who shot me was in a green terrifying bush. I handled my Uzi and fired to the bush. I realised this was about a lot more things as I fell to the cold sand. The gentle wind blew. I slowly closed my eyes; my life passed like a flash before me. Sweet music was heard from on high. The old world had gone, there would be no more pain …

Matias Eraso (13)
St Brendan's College, Buenos Aires

I Don't Want To Be A Princess

Last summer a group of Argentinean girls were invited to visit a castle located in Great Britain. The girls felt happy, waiting for their trip, imagining they would feel, for the first time, like princesses living in a castle.

Finally the girls departed for England. When they arrived they were led to the castle. Even though they felt tired, they decided to visit every corner of the place, except for one of the rooms located in the tower, because the door was locked.

After supper the servants who served the girls left the castle. As the girls felt tired they decided to go to sleep.

At midnight Mary was woken up by a strange noise. As she was walking along the corridor she heard a young woman's voice screaming and asking for help, which came from the tower.

Mary ran upstairs and tried to open the door. She remembered it was locked but when she turned the door handle it opened and she heard a voice that said, 'You and your friends must leave this castle now, if you don't want to be killed. I'm Anne Boleyn's spirit, one of King Henry VIII's wives. His spirit is in this castle and he wants to kill anyone who visits this place.'

Mary ran downstairs, woke up all her friends and told them what had happened. All of them decided to leave the castle that night.

Early next morning they decided to return to Argentina and thought that it was better not to be princesses.

Lisette Garcia Colomer (12)
St Brendan's College, Buenos Aires

The Black Knight

In London in 1432 there was a very well known knight who had a very particular armour. It was completely black and he rode a black horse. He was known in all of Europe because he never lost a battle. Every young man tried to defeat him but he was very strong, he killed every man who tried to beat him.

One day a boy called Charles started to train to defeat the black knight because he had killed his brother. His father was a blacksmith so he made him the best sword he could make to fight with the black knight.

After one year's training, he went to challenge the black knight. He went to the castle where he lived. He had a lot of problems getting there. The black knight was very intelligent. He set traps on the way to the castle. Charles had to walk through a forest full of tigers and beasts, and then there was a dragon at the door of the castle.

Charles was victorious and defeated the black knight, and was always recognised as the great white knight.

Juan Pablo Lechenet (13)
St Brendan's College, Buenos Aires

The Birds' Island

On a faraway and dim island there lived an old tribe called Bloomfield. They lived in a very comfortable way because there was complete peace and isolation. The members of the tribe's security was taken care of by their god, the Totem, who instead asked of them three conditions - being good humans, not idolising any other god and the most important, not making any type of damage to the exotic and coloured birds that coloured all the darkness of the sky.

Once when there was a shortage of food, the chief and a group of men decided to go fishing because they were starving, but they didn't choose the correct day. A big storm began in the middle of the Silon Sea. The sky exploded in light with a flash of lightning. The waves were enormous and the cold wind didn't let them go back.

The next morning their corpses were found on the coast.

Now they were in the position of having an election for the new chief of the tribe. It became a great issue of who would become the new chief. The election started and, although everyone knew that it was a real fraud, an old woman announced the result.

The new chief, Brutus, was a very sly man, so he became very dangerous for the tribe and the island too. Now that he had the opportunity of having the power, he would not miss the splendid opportunity. He decided to make new rules. Brutus persuaded people saying that it was not a sin killing birds and that the Totem would be happier if they took advantage of these creatures. After his speech he went on sleeping because he was fatigued but when he lay on the bed, a big bird with a red breast appeared and told him, 'Obey your god's orders!' and then flew away. Brutus shouted he was the authority and that he could do what he wanted.

After some hours Brutus woke up and found that all the members of the tribe were waiting for him dressed with the coloured feathers of the marvellous creatures. They were ready to eat the juicy birds. It was a delicious meal but it would be paid for very dearly. Everyone started feeling strange and an enormous blue wave appeared behind some trees. This was the tragic end of the tribe. It disappeared completely.

The powerful Totem converted the island into 'The Birds' Island' in the name of all the dead creatures.

Matias Soage (14)
St Brendan's College, Buenos Aires

The Red-Flowered Bag

She didn't even realise the repentine and dramatic change that that decision could have provoked. A broken family, loved one's heart broken … just thinking of it made her shiver. It was that drastic step that could have derailed the way of her life. She would have to run away, live in the big city, alone. That way she could pass unnoticed. That way they would never find her. That way she could live a normal life. But of course, she could *never* come back home.

In order to fulfil the plan, she would have to steal some money. Find a place to leave her burden this would have to be a place where she would never be found. Maybe a box in the river or in a basket on top of a tree. Somewhere unreachable. It couldn't be that bad, but of course, it would be a cruel thing to do.

Another difficulty to carry out her plan, was hiding it from him. If he found out, he wouldn't hang out with her. Their thing would be over. And of course, she wanted to keep him.

She wondered if anyone had noticed her growing tummy and her sudden mood change. She had already talked to her doctor. He had agreed to do it without telling her parents, but he had also told her that it was a very unwise thing to do.

Considering all things, she thought, her plan wasn't that bad. Maybe she should go on with it and miss her appointment with Dr Schwartz. Yes, she would do it and began packing her clothes in a small red-flowered bag.

María Paz Lucas (14)
St Brendan's College, Buenos Aires

The Worst Day

Today I woke up at 4.30am and went to work in a mill at 5am. Although I was very excited about it because it was my first day at work, when I entered the doors of the mill, the smell was intolerable.

My taskmaster told me to pick up the loose cotton that fell on the floor. At first, that seemed very easy, but then I realised that the noise of the machinery scared me and the dust made me sick. At 11am my legs hurt and I was starving; I had to wait till midday for a break.

At 1pm I had to go back to work. Then again, my taskmaster told me to pick up the loose cotton that was on the floor. I was very tired, I couldn't stand on my feet.

While I was doing my work, I heard lots of people shouting. I wanted to know what was going on. When I got near the place where the shouting came from I saw a boy that was trapped in one of the machines. The older ones were helping him to get out. When they managed to release him, he was still sobbing and he couldn't stand up, his legs were bleeding. I was shocked at the scene. I dreaded to think of what may happen to me. At 8pm, I finished working and went to the orphanage. I am quite sure this was the worst day of my life.

Maria Lucia Molina (14)
St Brendan's College, Buenos Aires

An Imaginary Life

Schizophrenia: a serious mental illness in which someone's thoughts and feelings are not based on what is really happening around them.

'John, they are not real!' That was what they kept on telling him, but he still couldn't believe it. All those years, all those people. He couldn't understand it. How was that possible? He was so real. Everyone was so real. He was mentally unbalanced by the thought.

The disease appeared while attending Princeton University. He was a maths student at the time. When John met Charles, he knew he was the perfect friend for him, but there was a problem with that, Charles wasn't real. For years they were friends and John never knew this.

Then Parcher came along, he wasn't a friend, but John thought he worked for the government, well he didn't, and he also wasn't real. Parcher made him believe that the United States required his mathematician skills. Apparently Russia was threatening the US and John could help. Everything became very complicated when Parcher told John that Russia was after him, because they knew he was helping the US.

Four years later John got married to Alicia. And she never realised what had happened to John. The problems didn't stop there. And Alicia started to ask herself questions she never did before. First, she wanted to meet Charles. And second, she began to realise that John was constantly afraid of someone she never knew, Parcher.

'The worst thing about schizophrenia is never knowing what is real and what is not'.

Cecilia Constanza Pisano (14)
St Brendan's College, Buenos Aires

The Crucial Day

She went to fetch my grandmother, to go to the hospital. She said she would call. It's 11am, my mother hasn't called yet. It all happened so quickly for her. No one is sure of what is going on inside Room 12. 11.05am, the doctors say that there is no turning back. He is getting worse. The last 20 minutes were crucial. My mother calls. Virginia arrives. My father answers the telephone. He runs out of the house and goes to the hospital. Virginia stays with my sister and I to look after us. The telephone doesn't ring.

Two hours later, my father, my mother and my grandmother arrive. My mother is riddled with pain. My grandmother goes to rest. My father and my uncle go to the funeral house. We are all oppressed by pain.

3.15pm, a gust of silence at home. Our faith falls to pieces over our souls. Pain resuscitates.

My father returns with the time of his burial. Tomorrow would have been his birthday. We will lock ourselves in the chapel praying for his loss.

Lost in the silence of love.

Julieta Canessa (14)
St Brendan's College, Buenos Aires

He

The first thing you noticed about her, were her eyes. She had beautiful green emeralds with a glimpse of curiosity in them. They were a shocking pair accompanied by her extraordinary golden hair. She was perfect in every single way and nobody could deny that. Nobody.

She was the cheerleader's captain, but she wasn't a stupid bimbo. She was the coolest girl in Ashtonville's junior high, but she wasn't a mean girl. She was what every teenage girl wanted to be - flawless, simply perfect.

Virginia wouldn't meet *him* until her 16th birthday, when her dad would throw a huge party for her sweet sixteenth. That day, the world as she knew it, crushed down into a million pieces and her life was gone.

Who might have known that her parents weren't the happy couple they seemed to be? That her mother, the perfect housewife who always had participated in school projects and seemed to be very joyful, was now lying in a hospital bed, trying to survive the terrible beating that her husband had given her.

Unfortunately, she didn't survive. Mr Moore went to jail, Mrs Moore to the morgue and Virginia, she went to the orphanage.

She met *him* there and *he* was the only thing that kept her heart beating through years. She never said a word about *him* and slowly, very slowly, she became the Virginia everyone knew and who was friends to everybody. But she never forgot that the only person who had always been with her was *him* and for that she will always be grateful to *him*.

Tessie Sills (14)
St Brendan's College, Buenos Aires

The Blue Planet

'Can you tell us a story?' the two naiokies asked before they went to sleep.

'OK I will,' Grandpa told them …

'Once upon a time there was a blue planet in which existed trees with brown, long, resistant bodies called 'trunks' which also had little ones with some leaves like our golmenas but they were coloured green and soft. This blue planet also had a beautiful fluid called 'water' which gave colour to the planet and some had living beings of different colours and sizes called 'fish'. They also had big pyramids like our ships but these were brown coloured and they were rough. The big ones had their tops painted with a white colour. These were called 'mountains'.'

'And how did these mountains smell Grandpa?' the naiokies requested impatiently.

'Oh there isn't a smell to describe the mountains,' the grandpa said with patience. 'The 'paradise' was inhabited by beings of different shapes called 'animals' that acted on instinct. They fed on other ones and on the green, soft leaves. In all of these animals there was a special gift, 'conscience' - he could think about what was he doing.'

'So they must have been wonderful they would never commit any mistake,' the twin naiokies said.

'You know, you are completely wrong,' Grandpa said. 'They had conscience about the consequences of their acts and besides their gift they managed to break the natural balance of the planet. The legend says that in their advanced ages they created a device called 'atomic bomb' which had an incredible destructive capacity. And our hero Kael'thas was sent to the planet to prevent them from destroying their beautiful habitat.'

'I hope we never develop some device like that,' the naiokies said sadly.

Grandpa said, 'Don't worry; we will always have a Kael'thas …'

Ignacio Gonzalez (14)
St Brendan's College, Buenos Aires

What You Don't Want To Believe

She looked at the image the mirror gave to her. Deadly pale skin, dark hair as black as night and two beautiful emeralds, once doors to her soul, calmed and relaxed, now reflecting how nervous and hysterical she was. That's how she was.

The scars weren't reflected on it. They were in her brain. In her rational thinking and conscience of reality. Many people had offered her their help without being successful.

She couldn't understand it. Who was she? The one that tormented her so much. The one who got into her house and called her name.

'Amarantha.' A whisper that couldn't be heard made her turn so quickly that she hit a chair and fell.

A hand was holding to her.

'Leave me alone. Stop! Go away,' she said to the woman, who'd made her shout desperately.

She got rid of the pliers that hurt her arm and without thinking what she was doing, grabbed a very heavy-looking book and gave her a severe blow directly into her nape. Instantly she fell as though someone had hit her in the head and everything went black.

The sun filtered through the curtains and caressed her cheeks, causing her a slight tickle that after a while became bothering and woke her completely up.

How strange. The last thing she remembered was hitting the woman with a book. What had happened to her?

She didn't have time to answer that question. Although she was alone, the feeling of being accompanied was too strong to ignore it.

She got completely sure when a voice rose in the air. 'Amarantha.'

With a wild scream she caught the woman's neck. The pulse was more and more slight as she steadied her trachea.

It stopped. The irregular bump on her hand stopped. She was dead.

She dared to open her eyes. She had closed them unconsciously when suffering her fury attack.

When her emeralds saw the woman's face she preferred never having opened them. The woman. She was someone she knew very well - herself.

Natalia Lofiego (14)
St Brendan's College, Buenos Aires

Illusions

Television, that exposes various truths, can cause enormous life-shattering shocks for people. It can bring several beings out of their prolonged illusions.

Riya was an ordinary girl living with her parents in the UK. Her sister had been married and lived in the US, but her life had been destroyed when the Twin Towers were bombed. Riya, who had been talking on the phone to her sister only the day before, could not have imagined that she would have to see her own sister's death live on TV.

One day she met a man in the street. She fell in love with him at first sight. He was Mark, a very handsome and loving person. As their relationship grew serious, she realised that he was extremely generous and there was nobody as lucky as her to have met him.

Riya had just returned from Mark's house, but hadn't found him at home, when she switched on the TV for the first time after the devastating incident. Browsing through different channels suddenly brought her attention to 'Breaking News: Three Terrorists Arrested'. Some pictures were being displayed. A current began running down Riya's body. Her mouth and eyes were left wide open. The whole benevolence had just been an illusion! Mark was a bloody terrorist. She had been deceived so intensely.

Television, that exposes various truths, caused an enormous life-shattering shock for Riya. It brought her out of her prolonged illusions.

Mamta Aggarwal (15)
St Constantine's International School, Tanzania

Unwodipi

On a Monday morning, the 4th of May, the year I forgot; we moved to the place that we are living until now. It was the only house in the whole pantaloon town, which was still unoccupied. The house itself was huge, a mansion in fact. It had 15 rooms in general and it was magnificent!

The second day after we settled in, I started looking around, trying to get acquainted with the area, when I saw at the back of the house many roses clustered with no definite pattern; their colour very odd: they were black!

I started looking through them to find anything suspicious when I saw a molehill. I touched it experimentally and I felt the ground below me lift and go up and up and up! I wanted to scream but when I opened my mouth, no sound came out so I gave up trying to scream and sat on the ground which had surprisingly become concrete and started praying. Suddenly, I heard children shouting and I opened my eyes, for I had closed them, and looked around me and I saw some sort of a school!

I went in one of the classrooms, asked teachers who were present what they taught and they told me that this was a school of *discipline* and that all the children that I was seeing came from planet Earth and more were coming from the planets Mars and Saturn. I was told to sit down because I was among the chosen ones from the Earth to learn and later teach ther children manners. So, I went to a course of eight weeks learning the following: a) why and how children should obey parents; b) why and how children should obey school teachers and adults in general. It was a very boring course and many times in class my mind kept wandering back home to my mother and father; how they were taking the fact that I'd vanished into thin air.

After the eight weeks, I woke up one morning and found myself at home at the same rose bed still searching for suspicious things. So, I came to the conclusion that eight weeks in that place (Unwodipi - the unknown, wondrous discipline place) was in fact, one minute on Earth.

I still remember the teachings but should I go and teach other children? Who would believe me? And most importantly, was it an illusion or reality?

Mercy Grace Kisinza (14)
St Constantine's International School, Tanzania

My Life In Tanzania

It has been almost ten years since I have been in Tanzania; over those ten years I have had good and bad times.

In the beginning when I came here from Korea I was very surprised to see so many black people. It was the first time I had seen people of different colours. My aunt, who is a missionary here, would take my family to her church on the Maasai land. The Maasai ladies would come up to me and start pinching me. Ouch, huh! But they were not trying to hurt me, just rubbing to see if my skin would become black.

Later on though, I became more in touch with them and started to speak Swahili. I went to an international school in Arusha and made a lot of new friends. I have all types of friends - Asians, Americans, Europeans and Africans. Here in Tanzania there are people of different cultures and people of different religions: Hindus, Muslims, Sikhs and Christians. I have learned to know new cultures.

Now I am fifteen and I know Tanzania is a wonderful place. It has the most beautiful land and outstanding islands. The national parks are full of all kinds of animals that you have ever imagined. Mount Kilimanjaro and Mount Meru are just fantastic to climb. The air here is so natural. Tanzania is a very peaceful country, just great to spend your life.

I love Tanzania.

Yejin Cho (15)
St Constantine's International School, Tanzania

The Rescue

It was a sunny day, the sun throwing its rays through the window into my bed. Oh yes, I remembered, I was babysitting my little brother as my parents were going out for the day. I woke up, freshened myself, and walked down the stairs to help my mum pack the hamper with sandwiches, cocoa drink and apples for the day.

An hour had already passed since my parents had left to meet my aunt in the nearby town. I was all alone with my baby brother watching television and playing with him, when I felt like going out. Sensing the coolness of the cloudy day, I left my brother, who was occupied playing with his toys. I walked around the garden feeling the breeze pass through my hair, when I suddenly smelt something burning. The burning smell was intense and I looked around searching the source of the smell. When I saw the house, I stood numb; I was in that state for 30-40 seconds. When I regained my strength to move, I could not believe the house was on fire. My brother, I remembered! My brother was inside the house. I started crying, not knowing what to do. I remembered the old rug Mum kept in the garage. I ran to take it and I was ready to run into the house. The cry of my brother and his fear could be felt inside me. I wrapped the rug around me and ran into the house.

I found my brother sitting on the floor crying, his face red with tears. I picked him up and wrapped the rug around us, when we were safely covered, I headed towards the door. By the time I reached the door, I felt a burning sensation on my back. Ow! I was burning. I did not have the strength to move and could not carry my brother any longer.

'Wake up Tehreen, wake up!' my mom cried.

'Where am I? Where is my brother?' I was crying.

'You've had a bad dream,' said my mom.

Oh Lord, I was so relieved. That was the worst dream I've ever had.

Tehreen Dharamshi (16)
St Constantine's International School, Tanzania

The Boy Of Her Dream

It was cold and foggy when nothing seemed to be clear, then a young lady met a handsome young boy. It was love in each one's eyes that shone and sparkled. The fog had blocked the view of shyness as there was not much to stare about.

The young lady could not even say goodbye due to the shyness that she had, but the boy kept his word of love not bearing a second as she had gone out of the view.

For a long time she had thought of the dream that she had once had. She had thought of the dream to make her happy when she was sad, thinking that one day they would meet again as in fairy-tale stories. But it was just a dream that she had during her lifetime and only an image of memory could come to her mind, but as it disappeared and grew weak with one's mind of weakness it remained a secret for what lay ahead.

All that was in her mind was the shining of the eyes as they sparkled with love and all she could think of was a beautiful dream of the stars at night, sparkling with love, as if she had once again met the boy of her dreams in a strong feeling.

Fahima Abubakar (15)
St Constantine's International School, Tanzania

A Simple Story

It was an ordinary class like any other when Jack was in school. It was athletics, he really hated running, but he was very fit.

It had just finished and he felt he had put something dreadful and boring behind. Just then a beautiful Indian girl passed him. At first sight all he thought was that she was very pretty. But he didn't know what was going to happen the very next day.

School had started at 7. The thing that also disturbed him was that he wasn't very bright. But this didn't worsen his life in any way. He thanked God that he was like that.

When school was over that beautiful, mystical Indian girl walked up to him and asked for his number, as he was clumsy with numbers he was a little nervous, but said it calmly.

Her name was Kiyo, it seemed a strange name but it didn't matter to him.

As he knew he had mistaken the numbers so he got her number from a friend and wrote a note to her saying, 'What's up! It's Jack, sorry I gave you the wrong number, anyway, just saying hi'.

She seemed to reply immediately to his surprise. So they went on talking about life, boyfriends, girlfriends and all. They were both single.

After a few days he got up the courage to ask her out. She took about three days but eventually said yes.

Frederic Marschall (15)
St Constantine's International School, Tanzania

Man's Best Friend

Long ago when the dinosaurs died, dogs came out of nowhere and started roaming around on the Earth's surface and enjoying themselves. They had an IQ of 100%.

Later, they found out that a certain god invented them. They thought that the god was a certain stone so they started worshipping it.

The Alsatians were the most devout dogs. They kept warning other dogs about a war that would occur years later. Only the Dobermans believed that because they were ready to fight, they were the bravest dogs. They believed anything about war. The Alsatians were also brave. The other dogs however, ignored the Alsatians incredulously.

The Alsatians were actually right.

200 years later, the Alsatians and the Dobermans suddenly started to kill each other in a quarrel over 'who are the bravest dogs on Earth?' No dog was able to separate the Alsatians and Dobermans.

The battle continued for years and years until humans came out of nowhere and broke the fight by telling them that they were both the bravest dogs. The battle suddenly stopped and the dogs thanked the humans.

As time progressed, the dogs IQ became 10% and the humans kept the dogs are pets.

This is why dogs are also known as 'man's best friend'.

Hiten Dave (11)
St Constantine's International School, Tanzania

The Creature …

A long time ago a creature known as Umbreon lived in the axe man cave in the land of Tajikistan. This creature had wings of a dragon, tail of a lizard and a face and body of a black wolf. The scariest part of the creature was the shiny three diamonds on his forehead.

Everyone who tried to kill him died, but there was one warrior who had the potential of killing him. His name was Chuchulian. He had the strength of 20 men. He was taller than a horse, broader than a cow. He bore an enchanted sword and shield. He was on a quest, a quest to kill Umbreon. He passed the town before the caves and rested there.

Then he left and disappeared into the early morning mist. He reached the caves at noon, had lunch and entered in.

After days of searching and mini adventures, he reached the den. Umbreon was sleeping. He woke him up. Umbreon woke up with a loud growl. He came out of his den and kicked Chuchulian. He fell with a bang.

Chuchulian got up and put on a great fight with Umbreon. They both started to get tired of fighting for hours. Then all of a sudden it struck Chuchulian to go underneath him and kill him. So he did. The creature growled which slowly faded away. He was the first person to come out of the cave alive.

Taher Muslim (14)
St Constantine's International School, Tanzania

Daydreaming In Summer

Sitting in class, I sat looking at the cutest girl and also popular in Midsburgh Middle School, Kirsten Myers. She had such sweet brown eyes and long chestnut-brown hair. I just kept drooling on and on.

Cring! The last bell of the day rang. I grabbed my bag and ran out of the classroom door. I hurried home, as fast as I could. I wanted to play my new game 'The Knights of the Dark'.

As I reached the porch, I threw my bag on the side. I ran upstairs to my room and switched on the computer. While it was loading a message appeared on the monitor, 'Your day has come'. I thought that this was a prank but it reappeared, 'It is Montonia, Knight of the Dark, I have come to you, to go to the other side, the land of Knighthood!'

I felt something tingle all over my body, suddenly there was a flash of light. I found myself on my back, staring at the blue clean sky. On my side I saw trees and huts and smoke. When I got up I saw a knight, coming from a short distance on horseback. I greeted him, he said, 'I'm Montonia, Knight of the Dark.' Something clicked, it was him, the one who brought me here. He continued, 'I have come to seek your help, Princess Kirstenia, has been kidnapped by the evil Duke Ederman.'

I jumped on his horse and headed to the castle. On our arrival, we went straight to a large room. Inside were knights and King Merki. He begged me to retrieve his daughter and I accepted. I was given the directions, my armour, sword and horse.

I set off west of the kingdom in my shiny armour. I reached a canyon, just as the directions said. I stopped, went through a crack with a staircase leading. I reached a wall, I tapped it and it flung open. There sat a beautiful pretty … *Kirsten!* I couldn't believe it, it was her. But I kept hearing someone calling me. 'Marcus! Marcus!' Who was, till I heard a whack!

'Ouch!' I yelled. 'What was that for?'

'You have been daydreaming about Kirsten again!' This time it was Katie whacking me in the head. Oh God, I couldn't believe that. It seemed so real. Oh OK I may get my chance with her at this upcoming summer dance.

Brita Masaua (14)
St Constantine's International School, Tanzania

A Four-Year-Old Baby Burnt To Death

A young baby aged four years old who did not know anything was killed by a house help. It all started as an argument between the owner and the house help, because the house help was not doing work that was expected. She was not cleaning the house, the food was not well cooked and sometimes it was even burnt. When the owner was talking to her she said she wanted to go home. She did not want to continue with the work. The owner told her she would give her her money tomorrow.

The following day when she went to work she told the house help she would bring her the money when she came home for lunch knowing that her daughter was still asleep. It reached around 11.40. She called through the landline asking if the child was awake and she said she was taking her tea. When the child finished taking her tea she kept the oven on and put the baby inside and she went to get her bag. The baby was crying for help but she did not do anything about it. No one was nearby who could help the young baby.

It reached around 1.30. The mother came in. When she entered the house she smelt something like roast meat, then she called the house help but no one answered. She thought maybe she had gone outside when she went to the kitchen she opened the oven and found her daughter burnt to death and the house help was not there.

This is possibly the worst thing a human being can do to a small creature who does not know anything.

Melba Jackson (14)
St Constantine's International School, Tanzania

Magical Football Feet

Mike Brown, the 17-year-old footballer who is known to be able to kick a ball so hard and fast that it can change or lose its shape, and is said if he kicks it against a wall depending on how hard he kicks it can pop the ball and even break the wall or devilishly hard metal.

He said he never knew his foot had so much power and says he doesn't know whether his left foot could make such a kick. He said he never knew what he could do and what he can do next. Maybe he could be a legend with his amazing kicks. He claims he began playing when he was only 7 and 17 is when he found out about that special talented kick. His coach is his dad, all his life he has been the only coach, and he practised every day for about 3 hours.

Mike hasn't been noticed much but has dreamed of being in the World Cup and entered for the English Premiership, UEFA Champions League, FA Cup and more. He aims to improve his father's grocery and sports equipment shop, with the money that he is going to be earning from his football career. He's also going to pay for his own university studies. Mike is now seen as one of the most promising footballers and with the best and fastest kicks.

Football clubs are now welcoming Mike with open arms and would want Mike to play for them. Every club is begging for Mike as their main star player in attack, left and right wing and their midfielder. Now we're waiting for Mike's next move.

Samson Reuben (13)
St Constantine's International School, Tanzania

Trapped In A Hole

It was a foggy afternoon when my friend and I set off to walk. We had to talk about our science project that Miss Jenefer had given us, as we were partners. She started explaining to me about the introduction. She talked about the designs. When I was about to tell her which book to look in for pictures she was not watching where she was going and she got stuck in a hole. Her leg turned at a bad angle and she got a fracture.

The hole was a trap for an animal, it was for rabbits, hamsters and other small animals. Not so far away there was a cottage where an old man lived called Mr Benet. He told me that the hole was a trap for small animals. He also told me that he had put in sharp nails so if the animals ran into the sharp nails they would die immediately.

Mr Benet stayed with my friend and I went back to town. At 12pm I reached town. I went to my friend's place and I told her mum what had happened. She got so worried and she called the rescuing department. They reached us at 12.15. We all rushed back to the forest, which we reached at 12.30. My friend's mum could not bear to see this but just for her daughter she stayed for as long as it took.

I took a piece of cloth and covered it in front of my friend's face so she would stop talking and thinking about it. It took us more than 6 hours because the ground was wet and slippery, and it was difficult to see where to dig because the rescuing department were scared of hurting my friend. My friend waited patiently till her leg was out. When her leg was out, she was taken to the hospital. The next day I went to meet her and she told me that she would not forget that day.

Sabiha Fazal (12)
St Constantine's International School, Tanzania

In The Kalahari Desert

In the middle of the Kalahari Desert, there lived two families. Both the families had sons. The first family, the Wachunga's son's name was Kilaan, while the second family, the Wangaruba's son's name was Ranaf.

One hot day, the two of them who were really good friends, decided to go for a walk. They walked for about an hour till they reached a small town. As they saw the town's buildings and the number of people, they were amazed because they had never seen them. Finally it was time to go home as the sun was setting.

Kilaan asked Ranaf, 'Do you remember the way we came?'

Ranaf said, 'No.'

As they were trying to remember the way back, darkness fell on the two boys in the middle of a town. They decided to sleep outside a big building before continuing to find their way back.

At home both the parents were worried about where they had gone. No one knew. They decided to wait till the next morning.

In the morning as the building's owner woke up, he saw the two boys sleeping. He slowly woke them up and asked them where they came from. They explained to the rich man, he remembered that he had a worker who knew all the places in the Kalahari Desert. He told his worker to take them home.

As they reached home, their parents jumped with joy. They thanked the man and promised that they would never go anywhere without informing their parents.

Sajjad Sajan (13)
St Constantine's International School, Tanzania

The Haunted Kingdom

A long time ago, in the ancient times, one kingdom had a strange history. The kingdom was the Zarco Kingdom in Western Asia. The kingdom had a very clever king, King Sac, and a very beautiful queen, Queen Mary. However, their daughter, Princess Dorthi, was very mean and didn't care for anyone. She was very proud of herself.

Princess Dorthi was ripe for marriage. The king and queen were concerned about her marriage. Whenever they told the princess to get married, she would go away and would never listen.

One day she decided that the man who would pass her tests would marry her. The tests were very dangerous. The person would have to face 9 soldiers, 2 lions and a very horrible-looking and powerful beast who looked like a man but was an animal with big claws. Many men had tried this test but ended up being killed. The king and queen tried to stop this but didn't succeed.

There was a war between the Zarco kingdom and Zinc kingdom. After a few days the Zarco kingdom had won the battle but there was terrible news, King Sac had died. The princess didn't care about what had happened. She just continued with her test.

One day a very powerful prince came. He came and won the princess' tests. The princess married the prince but later that day the prince went to Princess Dorthi and left her forever because she had taken many innocent lives. The princess got mad and jumped off the tower and died. Queen Mary knew that the princess was dead but her spirit would be looking for the prince, so the queen cursed the princess that her spirit would never leave the castle and the castle went down into the earth. When someone goes to that place, he/she will hear the princess calling the prince to come back.

Bhavesh Chundawadra (14)
St Constantine's International School, Tanzania

Music Banned In Arabia

In a certain village near Mecca, in Saudi Arabia all kinds of music in the country wasn't allowed to be played. All youngsters were really unhappy. This happened on the 4th of March this year!

'Sean, my best artist, was on a show that night, many people attended his show. I was also there myself, when some policemen entered the building and took Sean offstage, everyone started screaming and running,' reported Yussa.

Other kinds of arts such as painting and writing were also banned in all schools in the same day. 'I wonder what they will ban next?' said Mr Hameed. 'We are tired of hearing of these bannings and also not grateful about some teachers who will lose their jobs'.

Most art students feel very bad about this. They say they are not going to get the careers they were hoping for. The banning ideas may help the government in some way but this really effects the music teachers and artists who are committed to the subject. This won't bring an income to the teachers and artists.

This may lead them to go into drugs to forget their careers, or the teachers won't have jobs for themselves.

Lilian Maro (13)
St Constantine's International School, Tanzania

Drinking And Smoking At A Young Age

It was a cool night. There was a warm ocean breeze. Paul, a very handsome, young boy, who lived with his parents along the coast of the Indian Ocean, surely didn't know what was to happen to him.

Paul, now a drunkard and a victim of marijuana, through the influence of a friend called John, a marijuana seller, was a helpful and hardworking young man.

That evening Paul left home with his classmate Peter. He told his parents he was going to sleepover and study at Peter's but Paul went to John's for a party. John's house was in the city where John's customers could easily reach him. The party was about the fun of alcohol, drugs and smoking marijuana.

There was a lot of music and everyone had a good time including Paul. Though John's neighbours were complaining about the noise.

It was at the time when Paul and everyone in the party was taken up by the drinks and smoking. No one really expected it but all of a sudden policemen stormed the house and arrested everyone.

Poor Paul had to go through 20 years imprisonment and his parents lost trust in him and punished him by stopping his studies. Still today Paul is a very poor, untrusted and lonely fellow.

From the story we see that when we mess up our lives with alcohol and smoking we pay for it until the day we die.

Fanuel Baldwin (12)
St Constantine's International School, Tanzania

What A Girl Wants

One day, a girl called Lucy, who was a journalist, went to Mexico City. While taking a picture, she did not realise that behind her was a huge, steep hole. She fell in it.

An actor, who was called Marco, tried to save her by catching her but they fell in the hole together. When they saw each other, they fell in love. They soon got married and went to Marco's country, France.

Marco's parents, Kathrin and Eric did not like their daughter-in-law, but had to cope with her. Very soon Lucy was pregnant, but Marco did not know. Eric took Lucy out of the house, because Eric did not want her in his house, and made her write a letter saying that she was going away and never coming back.

After some time, Lucy gave birth to a beautiful baby girl, and named her Samantha. When Samantha grew up, all she wanted was a father so she researched on him and went to Paris to look for him. She found out that he was engaged to a girl called Salina and had adopted a child called Fiona.

When she went to his house, he was very shocked, he had another daughter and got very angry. The daughter and the mother were also very rude to Samantha.

Marco was getting closer and closer to Samantha and started to miss Lucy very much. He eventually decided to leave Salina and went back to his old family where they happily lived in Newcastle where Samantha and her mum lived before.

Lamiyah Khanbhai (12)
St Constantine's International School, Tanzania

Sarah And Her Worried Friend

Once upon a time there was a girl called Sarah, she was about 18 years old and when she was 16 she started driving. She drove into a gate the first week she started driving, then the second week she crashed onto a pole but was lucky nobody was injured. When she got home she had tears in her eyes and when her mother asked where she was she ran upstairs and shut the door. Her mother was confused and rang her friend. Her friend's name was Geesha. Geesha was her friend since primary and they both were in the same college. Her mother asked Geesha why Sarah was so upset but Geesha had no clue.

Geesha came home after an hour and talked to Sarah. Sarah was very upset but told Geesha the whole story. Geesha was very worried and so was Sarah. Both of them were thinking what to do but couldn't think of anything. Sarah told Geesha not to tell her mum because if her mum got to know she would not allow her to drive anymore. Geesha promised that she wouldn't tell her mother but … her mother was listening to everything from behind the door …

Henna Yusufali (12)
St Constantine's International School, Tanzania

Conquering The Holy Grail

'A chalice holding the blessed blood of Christ, shining in the moonlight, giving an appearance of royalty'. I had a vision that the lost chalice used during the last supper was found. But it was not to be. Though there was an atmosphere cheering and encouraging King Arthur and his knights to conquer it.

I watched through the window as they were dining. So I, Genevieve, decided to go along, though it would be disapproving to my parents and very rare for a woman to do so. But the spirit and fame had taken over me. So I hid among the reserves which were being carried in a cart.

When I first took a peep, I saw King Arthur tackling an intense situation at the Round Table. But then I saw that he was appreciating Galahad, commenting, 'You shall achieve that which no knight has achieved.' I fell in love with Galahad that very instant but revealing my presence would not benefit anyone.

But to my misfortune, Sir Galahad found a shrivelled creature battling the blistering cold. That creature was me. But he did not reveal my presence to the other knights. His words of advice struck me pots of gold. He advised me to get back into the cart silently. So I did, though heavy heartedly.

Throughout the whole trip, I did not get a glimpse outside, except for irritating moths and mosquitoes. We came to a halt in front of the hall. People were celebrating their success. But I was overjoyed when Sir Galahad announced that he was getting engaged to me. The royalty and the commoners were astonished. But King Arthur supported him.

The recovery of the Holy Grail was emphatic in the history of Britain, reuniting bravery with religious existences.

As Britain grows towards success in economic and social relations, one should not forget that its roots truly belonged to the legendary King Arthur and his brave knights.

Jovita Pinto (14)
St Joseph's School, Abu Dhabi

A Day In The Life Of My Great Grandmother, Mrs Devakiamma

(An extract)

Thin, slender figure, long hanging ears, wrinkled face and a bright toothless grin draped in a two-piece handloom mundu was how my great grandmother, Mrs Devakiamma would greet us during our trips to my grandfather's house in Kalady, Kerala. My mother was her youngest son's daughter and so I had a special place in her heart. The day we were to reach Kerala my achamma would stand near the gate, waiting impatiently for our car. On spotting it she would run and welcome us, shouting to others in the house, 'They have arrived, they have arrived!' She would then engulf us in her arms and kiss us all. This was how our vacation trip to Kerala began every year!

Whenever there was a function in *Puthen Veedu* (the family house name) it would seem like the entire town was there. My achamma has 7 children, many grandchildren and many more great grandchildren and whenever the entire family gathered it was so much fun. My grandfather is her youngest child and my mother is her favourite grandchild, and hence she had this special kind of love reserved for me, her great grandchild.

She had such long earlobes that would touch her shoulders, my hand could easily get through her ear hole! In olden days long earholes meant a sign of grace and status I was told and I always used to make fun of her by playing with her ears.

Achamma's day would start at 5.30 when she would have her bath and then come to the veranda and do her stretching exercises. She would then wait for one of her grandchildren to come and read out the main news from the newspaper for her. At 99 years of age she found it too difficult to read on her own. She would give her own comments based on the world news and talk about her days and now. This was the time she would talk about the freedom struggle of India and her active participation in it, she would also compare the rising costs of living during her times and now. She would have her breakfast which consisted of kanji (rice porridge) or anything liquidised as she had trouble chewing on anything hard.

In the afternoons she would gather all children and teach us how to make watches, whistles, spoons and other toys from leaves. She also took pride in making brooms from coconut leaves and then distributing them amongst her family members. My achamma was a constant source of inspiration for others by being fiercely independent and, in spite of having domestic help, she would wash her own plate and clothes.

Though she is no longer with us she still holds a special place in our hearts!

Neha Nambiar (11)
St Joseph's School, Abu Dhabi

Through The Eyes Of A Beggar Child ...

I stood there outside the bakery shop, peering through the glass to see a glimpse of those delicious, hot breads. My salivary glands now fully active; my nose just wanting a sniff ...

I had not eaten for the past 3 days. Dressed in rags and barefoot, I wandered all around the streets, hoping that someone would feel my pain. Finding absolutely no sympathy, I reluctantly made my way home; not to get a warm hug of consolation from my mother, but to see my drunk father beating her up; and my 2-year-old brother crying in the corner. I could bear it no longer, so I picked up my brother and vanished into the twilight ...

The survival of the night was the greatest challenge I faced then. Not for me, but at least for my brother I had to find food. I foraged the garbage bins and finally gasped, 'Thank You Lord, You are very kind,' on finding a small pack of biscuits with hardly one or two inside. I ate a quarter of it myself and fed the rest to my brother. The night was harsh and cold, but God had blanketed us under His care and love and we took shelter under a tree.

Morning; I picked up my poor, ailing brother and set out for the streets. I went begging from bus to bus, car to car; each and every vehicle, but all I had earned was 3 rupees and a lot of mocks. My whole body screamed out to me in anguish. But, God had not left me; I managed to buy a piece of bread. The happiness this little piece gave was much beyond euphoria. I quickly took some of it and fed it to my brother; and just as I was going to bite it, I saw a young girl, in the same shoes staring at the bread. Willingly I gave her what I had and left.

Crying only in my heart, my stomach had been empty for 4 days. My lips were parched from pain and thirst and with each step that I took, my body grew weaker and fainter. The only thought that dominated me now was my brother. Finding no other option, I left him at the door of an orphanage; only praying that he'd never see a life as that of mine; ever.

I was on my own now. Not knowing where to go, I entered a 'Saraswati Temple' nearby. As I was considered 'unclean' I was not allowed inside, so I sat near the steps, closed my eyes and cried. My heart was just about to blame God when suddenly I remembered my close friend who had been sent for prostitution by her father for money. At least I was better off.

My body now had no spark of strength left in it. Evening passed, I still didn't leave the temple. I felt my breath abandoning me. I couldn't wait to go to Heaven. I was sure to be welcomed by a warm hug and some food from God.

In the next instant, everything blacked out. I had reached my destination, I was in God's arms ...

Anjana Thomas (17)
St Joseph's School, Abu Dhabi

Friendship Policies

Hi! I'm Amy and you might probably be wondering what this story is all about, right? It is my own, what I have experienced, so I promise I won't make it boring at all. Now, let's see, my story …

Friends are people who I have always wanted, since I was always left out. Blame it on me for not going to them, but I was really shy. Once I was approached by a girl of my age. She was sweet and I soon began to like her. She was sincere and loving and I soon forgot all my worries. Oops, I forgot to tell you her name, it's Ann. Our friendship grew until it could no more, but I thought of her as the centre of the universe. We were like best friends and I didn't even care to go with others. Why should I?

It was all well until graduation, for then I started to like other girls for their cool dresses, money etc. I went with them and they too acted like friends. I know I was stupid but that was my age. I started to leave Ann out and go with my so-called friends. Ann didn't even complain but I was sure she was very sad. These friends forced me to give parties and neglect my studies. What could I do?

Then, one fine day, my so-called friends left me 'cause I dressed so uncoolly. I was heartbroken and there came Ann to my comfort. I realised the true meaning of friendship and here I am with my friend Ann. I have only one thing to say, 'A friend in need is a friend indeed.' Realise it before it's too late.

Smera Manoj (11)
St Joseph's School, Abu Dhabi

A Day In The Life Of Hilary Duff

Oh God, I'm so tired! I thought as I sat down to rest. *Being a star is great and everything but as soon as I do something out of place like sleeping over at a guy friend's house, rumours will start spreading that my friend and I are dating or something gross. Now there's a rumour that Lalaine and I are in a huge fight and we're not talking to each other except when filming the series. Magazines would do* anything *to get their ratings up.* I was so caught up in thought that I didn't notice that it was time to start filming again.

I looked up and saw Jake waving his hands to get my attention.

'Hello? Is there anybody there?' Jake asked, flailing his hands more vigorously.

'Oh! Sorry. I was just thinking about something,' I said apologetically.

'Yeah. I could tell when I saw that frown on your face, so I decided to check if something's wrong.'

'No, it's nothing,' I said reassuringly. When I saw the concern on his face, I insisted, 'Really! It's nothing at all!'

'If you say so,' he said doubtfully. 'If you're thinking that being a star is terrible, try to put a little optimism in your thought. You could make a huge difference in the lives of your fans. Think about it, okay?'

'Sure,' I said.

He walked away.

I thought about it and tried to think about the good stuff. I realised that Jake was right and I could really make a difference. Life is not so bad after all. It's *great!*

Dona Veronica Javier (12)
St Joseph's School, Abu Dhabi

Wealth Brings Happiness - A Myth

Money and wealth can bring happiness in our lives. Well, that's a present day myth. Pondering on this, an overly simple answer which strikes my mind is - sure, wealth brings happiness if it's rightly earnt and no if it's earnt through dubious means.

Does money buy us happiness? Would a little more money make us a little more happier? At this question, many of us smile and nod, because there is, we believe, some connection between fiscal fitness and a sense of feeling fantastic. Making it big brings temporary joy, but having it doesn't guarantee happiness.

So, believing that a little more money would make us a little happier, are we today, with our increasing affluence, more happier? No. It's a fact that individuals who strive most for wealth tend to live with a lower well being.

In Western countries and Japan for example, sharp increases in the percent of households possessing all modern amenities has not been accompanied by increased happiness.

Hence, what's the point in accumulating all the luxuries of life, closets full of seldom-worn clothes, garages with luxury cars all purchased with a vain quest for happiness that is elusive? Further, is there any justification in leaving enormous inherited wealth to one's heirs, as if it could buy them happiness, while on the other hand, the same wealth could do much good in this miserable world?

So, let's transform ourselves and also change this myth - 'Wealth brings happiness' to *'Wealth brings happiness only when it is spent for a good cause'*.

Fernon D'Costa (16)
St Joseph's School, Abu Dhabi

A Day In The Life Of My Mother

If there is someone in this world who is great, takes care of me and is an important person in my life - it's my mother.

A day in the life of my mom begins as early as five o'clock in the morning. Getting up from bed, she rushes through the chores of preparing a morning breakfast for me and my siblings and takeaway snacks for us to eat during school recess. When we pack our bags and rush to board the school bus, she's always there to tell us 'bye', that wonderful 'goodbye', one which I would cherish all my life.

My mom is a working woman, who works in a busy office. After we go to school she goes to work and returns in the afternoon only after we are back and had our lunch. After having her lunch she helps us with our homework and studies. She prepares nice food for us too.

My mom and I spend a lot of time together. In the evenings we make our school projects together and have lots of fun making arts and crafts. Sometimes we all go to the shopping mall to spend time buying clothes and then we eat at the restaurant. My mother enjoys gardening and spends some time each day taking care of her plants.

After a hectic day, when we children go to bed, she continues with her household chores till it's time for her to retire. So this is a typical day in the life of my mother.

Shannon D'Costa (11)
St Joseph's School, Abu Dhabi

Disguising Someone

Once upon a time there lived two girls in Canada. Their names were Ann and Sally. They studied in Ninth Grade in Jellystone High. They both had blonde hair, green eyes and looked the same, but their styles were different. Ann's best friend was Amy and Sally's best friend was Lila. Both Ann and Sally were members of a spy group in their school.

One day a new teacher came to their school. She was their class teacher. Her name was Miss Cathy. She was very kind on the outside but her heart was filled with hatred. She only liked the twins. Miss Cathy taught them science which was the twins' most favourite subject. Miss Cathy's real name was Suzy. She was one of the most wanted criminals in Canada. She was also very dangerous. No one knew who she really was because she had such good behaviour.

A week passed and Miss Cathy did not come to school. When the twins reached home their mom called out to them, 'Ann, Sally, there is a letter for you.' Ann ran and got the letter from the hall and opened it. The letter said, 'Beware, someone is going to be missing in your family soon by Zyx'. Ann was shocked and told Sally. They both knew either of them was going to be missing. The next day they got another letter which said, 'Come near the clock tower at 5pm today'.

The twins reached the clock tower at 5.05pm. They were looking for the villain when suddenly Ann got a huge blow on her head and she screamed. After a few minutes Sally was searching for Ann but couldn't find her.

After a few hours Ann found herself in a dark room. Sally went home quickly and called the police. Ann had a mobile so she called Sally and told her that she was kidnapped, tired and locked up at the back of the clock tower. Sally, the police and the spy club went to the clock tower later that day. Suzy was caught and Ann and a few other children were saved. For catching Suzy, the twins, spy club and Jellystone High were rewarded 2,000 Canadian dollars by the President of Canada.

Elizer D'Silva (13)
St Joseph's School, Abu Dhabi

All's Well That Ends Well

Carlisle ran lightly over the green grass, her movements exuded charm and grace. She called me to come and join in her playful caper, but I settled down more comfortably in the shade. Finally she came to me and said, 'Come, let's go back to the house, I've got to complete my research.'

Carlisle had just finished a course in cardiology. Now she was applying for a job, but it seemed that lady luck had forgotten her. Her parents had opposed her decision to become a cardiologist. They felt it would be a very difficult job for her, so they wanted her to join the family business, but Carlisle was firm about her decision. The situation in the house was very tense.

When we reached home, Carlisle's mom was preparing dinner and her dad was in his easy chair, jumping channels on the TV. So we went upstairs to her room. There Carlisle sat down with her research and I sat on the bed and watched her. I admired her like a lover admired his beloved. I worshipped her like a devotee worships his god. She was the centre of my world. My whole life revolved around Carlisle. She had shown me what love and kindness were and I was indebted to her.

Next morning we woke up to bright sunshine and the smell of snappers and eggs. We went down to breakfast. Carlisle's dad had traded his easy chair for the kitchen counter stool and his TV for the newspaper. Her mom was at the stove cooking breakfast, but there was a certain affectedness in their manner. Carlisle's mom said as casually as she could, 'Dear, there's a letter for you.' Carlisle practically grabbed the envelope from the counter. She took out the folded bit of paper with bated breath, read it and screamed with joy. She had been accepted at the Bellevue Hospital. Thousand watt smiles found themselves on her parents' faces. There was the hugging and blessing and then she picked me up and danced with me around the room.

'Romeo, here's your milk,' said a happy Carlisle. I purred happily and lapped up my milk. I thought of the Bard's play, 'All's well that ends well'. And that was our happy ending.

Melissa Fernandes (16)
St Joseph's School, Abu Dhabi

Story About A Girl That Really Touched My Heart

The place was in Baghdad, Iraq. It was a cold winter; a girl was living with her family in a house not far from a river called Dija. Her father was earning his living and supporting his family by selling some kind of local food to passers-by and tourists.

They hailed from northern Iraq. Her mother went to visit her family in a town called Kirkuk and after a few days the war broke out in Iraq. That was in 2003, her mother was not able to come back to Baghdad as there was fierce fighting. So this girl was acting like a mother to her younger brother and sister and looking after them, washing them and feeding them. It was a hectic time for the girl, but she has no other choice, being the eldest in the family and in the absence of her mother she carried on with the housework. Of course, the school was closed because of the war. Her mother tried to come to Baghdad but the road which led to Baghdad was closed to civilians. She worried so much about her children and everything got out of her control. In the meantime, she could not bear all that was happening to her and her family, she collapsed and died.

Her family in Baghdad did not know what had happened to their beloved mother. They could not call her on the phone as the telephone lines were not working in the whole country; they were not able to communicate and they kept wondering what had happened to her ...

Hiyab Yohannes (12)
St Joseph's School, Abu Dhabi

A Day In The Life Of Little Andrew

Little Andrew came into the kitchen where his mom was making dinner. His birthday was coming up and he thought this way was a good time to tell his mother what he wanted. 'Mom, I want a bike for my birthday.' Little Andrew was a bit of a troublemaker. He had gotten into trouble at school and at home.

Andrew's mother asked, 'Do you think you deserve a bike for your birthday?'

Little Andrew, of course, thought he did. Andrew's mother wanted him to reflect on his behaviour over the last two years. 'Go to your room Andrew and think about how you have behaved this year. Then write a letter to God and tell him why you deserve a bike for your birthday.'

Little Andrew felt very sad and he hated it when his mother was right. So he went upstairs to his room and wrote a letter to God.

Letter 1 - 'Dear God, I've been an OK boy this year. Please can you send me a bike for my birthday? Make it a red one. Andrew'.

Andrew knew he couldn't send this letter so he wrote a second letter.

Letter 2 - 'God, I know I haven't been a good boy this year, I am very sorry. I will be a good boy if you just send me a bike for my birthday, please! Andrew'.

Andrew knew even if it was true, this letter was not going to get him a bike. Now Andrew was very upset. He went downstairs and told his mom that he wanted to go to church. Andrew's mom thought her plan had worked, as Andrew looked very sad.

'Just be home in time for dinner,' said his mother.

Andrew walked down the street to the church and up to the altar. He looked around to see if anyone was there. He bent down and picked up a statue of the Virgin Mary. He slipped the statue under his shirt and ran out of the church, down the street, into the house and up to his room. He shut the door to his room and sat down with a piece of paper and a pen. Andrew began to write his letter to God.

Letter 3 - 'God, I've kidnapped your mother, if you want to see her again, send the bike! Andrew'.

Asha John (13)
St Joseph's School, Abu Dhabi

Myths And Legends

The word myth is often mistakenly understood to mean fiction - something that never happened, a made-up story or fanciful tale. Myths tell only of that which really happened. This does not mean that myths correctly explain what literally happened. It does suggest, however, that behind the explanation there is a reality that cannot be seen and examined.

According to legend, Arthur was the son of King Uther Pendragon. Immediately after his birth, Arthur was given into the keeping of Merlin, the magician. Merlin took him to Sir Hector who brought the child up as his own son. After Uther's death Arthur proved his right to the throne by pulling out a sword that had been fixed in a great stone and which no one else had been able to move.

King Arthur married Guinevere and held his court at Camelot, which is also sometimes identified as Caerleon, on the River Usk in England, near the Welsh border. Around him he gathered many strong and brave knights. They all sat as equals about a great round table, and thus they ultimately came to be known as 'The Order of the Round Table'. King Arthur extended his conquests far and wide. The dissension appeared, his traitorous nephew Mordred, rose in rebellion. In a great battle Mordred was defeated and slain, but Arthur himself was mortally wounded. His body was mysteriously carried to the Island of Avalon to be healed. He was expected to return at some future time and resume his rule.

Reshma Mariam Georgi (11)
St Joseph's School, Abu Dhabi

Alien Encounter

Since 1945 an immense body of evidence has been growing to support the reality of UFOs. The walls of secrecy long maintained by governments to serve their own purposes may soon collapse under mounting pressure from scientists and ordinary citizens demanding to know the truth.

Several fast-moving objects appeared on radar scopes at 3 installations, including Andrews AFB. Bryan Tanner said, 'My wife and her friend stood in the backyard at about 8pm and witnessed a large, silent, hovering object with bright, multicoloured lights that strobed in a diamond-shaped pattern'.

People watched in amusement and dazed horror as the spaceship landed (in Australia). It didn't take them too long to start their mischief. They overturned vehicles, uprooted trees, shattered windows and broke open doors. Fearful shrieks and pitiable cries of the earthlings had filled the air. The aliens caused unabated chaos. Many people swooned on seeing the ghastly sights.

The government, meteorologists, news reporters and police chiefs thought of ways of putting their foot down. Soon, they were put into action. The firefighters caused fire on a large piece of land where the aliens were inhabited temporarily. The woodcutters and the weak hands of the farmers tried their best to plunge the aliens into the mouth of death.

At the eleventh hour, the spaceships had taken off and soon the flying saucers disappeared into the darkness of the clouds. Meteorologist, Gwen Irano reported, 'The chunky pieces of rocks used as fuel in the spaceship that was left behind on planet Earth implies that the aliens are descendants of planet Mars'.

The savage havoc played by the aliens will be remembered like a nightmare for the years to come as 10,500 people died.

Sonam Bhatia (15)
St Joseph's School, Abu Dhabi

The Legend Of The Lost Legend

We finally landed at the Kinhasa International Airport in Zaire, Africa, after a two and a half hour flight. The 3pm blazing sun burnt my skin, causing it to crack. My colleagues and I hurried to a hotel and checked in. I explored my room which was beautiful with a generous amount of space, and strolled onto the balcony. It was a beautiful sight. Alas, with my job I had no time for nature or its beauty.

You see, I was an archaeologist and my dream was to uncover the legendary 'lost legend' and strike it rich. Being so valuable, many had tried to uncover it but failed. What seemed most intriguing was the fact that these people - some being my fellow colleagues - went out in search of it and mysteriously never returned …

Greed brought me in search of the legend and after two years of research and loads of expenses, I took a plane to the Congo a few days later. I was in my new room just going through my papers before setting out on my great expedition. The last bit of information that we had found out was that the box containing the legend had an unfamiliar sign on it. Contained in it was a beautiful flower. Legend says that this flower belonged to the most beautiful girl in the Congo. It seems she was very much disliked by her mother-in-law. The girl used to plant this flower in her garden. The flower was said to have golden petals with a tinge of black in the centre, and magically the flower never died even though it was plucked. The mother-in-law became suspicious and wanted to get rid of her daughter-in-law. Hence she made up a story that the girl was unfaithful towards her husband and as a punishment she was locked up in a tiny room.

Before her death, in revenge, the girl inscribed a curse on one of the petals of the flower and locked it in a jewel-encrusted box.

This box was supposed to be guarded by some nomadic tribe known locally as 'Masai'. This tribe village was located near the river Ubangui. My friends hired a local boat that would take us there.

We reached the Masai-inhabited jungles. Cautiously, we set off on foot on a single path that led to the village. The place felt like a bubble, the air was unusually quiet. Then all of a sudden, a huge rumble tore through the jungle. At a distance there was a crowd of Masai warriors running towards us. They encircled us with their sharp spears pointing at our throats. At the sound of a loud trumpet, all the warriors fell to their knees and the chief walked towards us. He was an imposing man with a face painted half black and white, and a crown of the peacock feathers.

I immediately asked him if he knew anything about the 'lost legend'. He happily spoke to his guards and they ventured off into the village area. They returned momentarily with a box in their hands.

The overwhelming joy that swept over me made me shake. What would people say when I went back a famous man? I looked up and saw the villagers had started to pack and were beginning to leave. Well, I had no time to ask them where they were going for I had to open the box. And so I did, and in it was the most beautiful flower I had ever seen. I was in tears. I took out the flower and on its petal, in iconic writing was written *'Thou that owns the lost legend, shall be lost forever ...'*

I laughed and thought it was a joke, but suddenly the jungle appeared unfamiliar. I read the curse again and realised what it meant, I was lost forever!

Manassa Rebello (15)
St Joseph's School, Abu Dhabi

A Day In The Life Of Britney Spears

I stood, perplexed, in front of my manager, my fingers clasped tight on a single sheet of newspaper smashed to pulp, early one Sunday morning. 'What is this supposed to mean?' I yelled in his pale face.

He sighed and slowly rose from his chair. 'Britney, Britney, Britney.' He scanned quickly through the article and looked patiently into my eyes. 'You know it isn't true. Why do you let the press annoy you like this?'

I drew in a long, shaky breath and squeezed my eyes shut. I just needed a minute to get over these stupid rumours.

'Britney!'

I clenched my jaw in frustration. What now?

'MTV's waiting, you have to move now if you want to make it to the photo shoot at 5.00, the interview at 8.00 and don't forget the concert preparations.'

Within a second I was dragged out unmercilessly to get changed. Once in my dressing room, I glanced at the thousands of outfits laid out. I went through all of them, exasperated.

Everything was wrong. My hair was tangled and uncontrollable and to top it all off, three pimples popped out of my face. No matter how much make-up or gel layered my face and hair, it was still not enough. What if the fans hated it?

Even if I wanted to, I couldn't change anything because just then, I was ushered out into a shimmering black car. The driver slammed his foot down and the vehicle zoomed off, with speed too high to even calculate, leaving me clutching onto the armrest for dear life …

Joanna Jayawickrema (12)
St Joseph's School, Abu Dhabi

A Day In The Life Of A Coin

Hey guys, I'm a beautiful, shining metal coin. I am obliged to know that you are eager to experience a day in my life, so, without wasting much of your time, let's carry on.

My active day of 25th March 2005 began when I was paid over the counter of a bank to a gentleman who cashed a cheque. I am a beautiful and distinct coin and am very proud of my smart appearance. Coming back to the point, I went off jingling in the man's pocket; but I was not there long, as he gave me to a shopkeeper.

The shopkeeper looked pleased when he had me in his hand and said, 'I have not seen a new coin for a long time.'

I was put in the drawer then.

Soon, I was in mixed company. I took no notice of the greasy coins as I knew they were of low caste; and I was condescending to the small change, knowing that I was twice as valuable as the best of them, but I found a number of coins of the same value. Most were old coins, dull and worn out. Some of them were jealous of my smart appearance and made nasty remarks. I cared the least.

I've no time to tell the fiftieth part of my adventures for the day. I have had an active day and hope you have had the same listening about it. Now, seeing my life would you like to live it?

Kavya Satish (11)
St Joseph's School, Abu Dhabi

The Trials Of Oedipus And Electra

Two important cases were to be heard in an Athenian court. Firstly, Oedipus' case came up. The judge questioned, 'You have been accused of killing your own father! Explain yourself!'

Oedipus replied, 'I was born to the King and Queen of Thebes. An oracle said that I would kill Father and marry Mother. So he pinned me to the ground in a forest. I was rescued and brought up by the King and Queen of Corinth. When I grew up, I learned from the oracle that the King of Corinth was not my father, but he was to me. So I fled to Thebes. I happened to kill a man on the way and later married the Theban queen. They turned out to be my real parents! It was not my fault, Fate.'

Then the judge summoned Electra, 'You have killed your mother! Defend yourself!'

Electra replied,' I was born to Agamemnon and Clytemnestra. While my father was at war, my mother had a lover. On his return my father killed him. My angry mother killed my father. To avenge my father's death I helped my brother Orestes in killing my mother. What I did was right!'

Then the defence lawyer requested of the judge, 'The accused have loved one parent and hated the other to the extent of killing them. These are deeds which no sane human would do. So I ask you to call upon a doctor to examine if they are mentally sane?'

After the examination the judge said, 'It is natural for a person to love one's parents. But to madly love one parent and kill the other is unnatural. It is an act of a person who is mentally unstable. As the doctor has found Oedipus and Electra to have such mental instability, I free them and put them in medical care.'

Meena Murugappan (11)
The International School of Lusaka, Zambia

The Nyami Nyami

Long ago deep in the heart of the Victoria Falls lived the 'Demon of the Waters'. Once you entered the waters you never came back. The locals chant their stories about this creature, the Nyami Nyami to their children as a warning. Calling like a crying baby, the Nyami Nyami drew mothers and daughters alike to the water to look for the 'child' in distress. Many villagers went missing as the creature called them to the waters. It acted every fortnight as the women gathered water for the village. The animal never came on to the land, the water was its hiding place. Ten metres of hulking, sleek, black leather, with large protruding fangs, it looked like a giant water snake and swam silently through the strong current.

One day the villagers got together and decided to go after the creature and kill it. They searched the whole river and found nothing, but how could such an enormous animal vanish? No one knew, but surely enough it struck again.

As hunters from far-off lands started to get curious about this hidden legend, the creature appeared less frequently and soon disappeared.

Today there have been many sightings of a giant black thing swimming at the bottom of the Victoria Falls, but with no verification. A few people have disappeared, but there has been no proof that the creature was to blame. Some people still hear the cry of a baby in the early mornings, but no one is sure, or even wants to find out, if it is the Nyami Nyami.

Catherine Mutazindwa (17)
The International School of Lusaka, Zambia

Teenage Romance!

It was the start of the summer vacation and Leanne always wanted to have a holiday romance. She didn't have much luck with long relationships, so she thought this would be ideal for her.

Leanne was a pretty, eighteen-year-old, blonde. It was a hot Friday night down Bar Street. The music blared from every bar, loads of clubbers, lights skimming the floor. As she walked into the bar, suddenly Leanne and Matt's eyes met across the crowded room. Matt was a tall, dark, handsome English-Cypriot. They exchanged a smile. He started walking towards her, introduced himself and asked her to dance.

At the end of the night they didn't leave each other's sides. Leanne gave Matt her number and was hoping she would receive a call the next day.

Morning came, but no call! Leanne waited and waited. Suddenly, her phone rang! It was a 'private number'. As she answered and heard 'hello', she knew it was Matt's sweet, kind voice. They arranged to meet that day to go to the beach. After they left each other, Leanne always got a phone call either that night or the next morning.

Matt and Leanne met every day of his vacation. She really thought this time he was the one!

The day of departure was agony. Tears flowed, her heart broke, he promised eternal love and to return soon. Leaving the airport she bumped into Matt's friends, 'I bet his wife-to-be will be glad to see him back! What a stag party!'

Emma Salatas (15)
The International School of Paphos, Cyprus

Ouija Boards

Some people believe they can connect with the spirits. One way of doing this is using a 'ouija board', the basic concept of which goes back in time to Pythagoras, 540 BC. He would send messages from the spirit world along with his student, Phlolaus. The modern board was invented in 1982 by two friends, E C Reiche and Charles Kennart.

A planchette was used as a pointing device, as it rested on a wooden lap tray with the numbers 1-10, the letters of the alphabet and the words 'Yes' and 'No' imprinted on it. The planchette moves around the board with your fingertips resting against it.

Ouija boards are used by two or more people, with your fingertip slightly resting against the planchette, ask a question aloud and wait. If you are serious about using the board and contacting spirits, some unusual things may occur. Some of these unusual things can be scary! In the past, it has been rumoured that someone had been thrown across a room for saying something wrong.

When the session is finished, place the planchette on 'goodbye' and say you are leaving. Treat astral entities the way you would want to be treated. Don't command; communicate. Be polite.

Ouija boards are not evil, they are cardboard and plastic. If you have had a bad experience, you should burn or throw it away. It's a controversial phenomenon; scientists and doctors just tend to look at hard facts, but who knows? When you die, are you actually gone? What do you think?

Laura Hudson (14) & Katie Zavros (15)
The International School of Paphos, Cyprus

Hera

Once upon a time there was a sweet little girl called Hera. Her father was the king of the land which made Hera a princess.

One day Hera was walking in the palace gardens when she felt something slither round her neck. She looked down to see a viper. 'Argh!' she screamed, but it was too late, the viper had bitten her with his deadly venom. She fell to the ground clutching her neck.

Her beautiful golden locks fell out and in their place deadly snake heads. She suddenly turned from a shy, sweet little girl to a horrible, ugly, evil monster. When the venom had gone into her it was bad venom and it turned her evil.

Knowing she wouldn't be able to live in the palace again she set up a home in a cave nearby. Although she could control her behaviour, she couldn't control her hair. Every time she went out the snake hair would bite someone for food.

A lot of warriors heard of her monstrous behaviour and set out to kill her. Most of them didn't succeed.

One day a handsome, kind soldier heard of Hera and knew the only way to cure her was not to kill her but to kill her 'hair'. So he set off to Hera's cave. After a long battle Hera turned back to her beautiful self. She moved back to her palace and married the handsome soldier and they lived happily ever after.

Amber Burrell (12)
The International School of Paphos, Cyprus

Herodus

On the twelfth night just before sunrise, Herodus awoke from his chamber startled. He saw nothing of his wife, she had disappeared! He searched and searched, but there was nothing to be found. He decided to take a rest so he went to sit on the kitchen table. He started to daydream when he spotted a note. He grabbed the note and read it. It said, 'Dear love, Herodus, The sun destroyed me. He's taken me as a sacrifice towards the moon. If I did not go with him he would have killed you. My heart would not take that and I would die! Goodbye forever my love, I love you, I love you, your dearest love, Maria'.

When Herodus read this letter he became furious and grabbed his bow and arrow and went outside to find the sun. The sun had not yet risen so what he did was wait and wait, and finally the sun came out! He grabbed his bow and arrow and shot towards the sun. The arrow went straight up into the sky and came straight back down, and landed in his heart.

His last words were, 'This has happened, I have died to come closer to you my love because I could never ever live without you.' He died peacefully in a field where lilies, his wife's favourite flowers, grew. The sun shone down on him, for now his life was about to begin with Maria his love.

Katerina Havouzari-Waller & Alice Bridges-Westcott (12)
The International School of Paphos, Cyprus

Penny Wise Foolish

Once upon a time there were two twins who weren't a bit alike in any way!

One of the twins Reena, was always up to mischief, stealing jewellery and constantly getting into trouble. Whereas the other twin Deena always helped he mother, made the dinner and everybody loved her. She didn't really get on with her twin sister. They had nothing in common at all, except they were relatives and they also shared the same birthday!

One day their parents had given them some pocket money, but it was rather a lot of money. Deena decided to spend some of it and then save the rest, just in case something more important happened and she needed the money, and she did actually need the money!

Whereas Deena's sister Reena, got very excited and decided to spend all the money in one go, without saving a penny.

She went into town and spent all the money on new clothes, magic creams, shoes, beads and some fruit.

She soon returned home and still had a smile on her face until she saw her parent's reactions. Her mother was in tears and her father was furious. They were in debt! Reena was so shocked and started to cry herself.

Deena saved the day though. She paid off the debts and her parents were so happy they elected her as the queen of the kingdom and Reena was green with envy.

Sophia Hackman (12)
The International School of Paphos, Cyprus

A Day In The Life Of A Tortoise

Yesterday was excellent! I woke up at about five in the morning to have my breakfast and a wash. I slowly walked towards my wash basin, then halfway there I decided it was all too much.

I lay down, put my head in my shell and began to sleep … *again.*

You see the only problem with my life is there's no action! (If you know what I mean.) It's just been me and this big old cage for nearly fifty years. Anyway, moving back onto my life story. While I was asleep I was awoken by this strange noise. It was the cage door being opened. Spam, my owner, put a little box in my cage, opened it, then shut it again. This really, really fit little tortoise started crawling out of the box.

All I could think to myself was, *finally, some action around here!*

I started to chat her up and we got know each other. Then we had lots of little baby tortoises.

Giles Newbon (13)
The International School of Paphos, Cyprus

The Tale Of Medusa: Reborn

Chapter 1

The archaeologists broke open the seal of the aged old tomb. They slowly crept down the cracked and worn paving and then stared around in immense suspense. As they came to the entrance, guarding the tomb were thousands upon thousands of snakes! They were trapped! Suddenly, one of the explorers whipped out a flame-thrower, incinerating the conniving little serpents that blocked their path.

They were free to waltz right into the tomb. They silently tiptoed to the tomb and slowly shifted the boulder aside, only to find that the creature was nowhere to be found! They heard a noise, a scream and then silence. The explorers were terrified, they rushed to the exit, trapped! The entrance had collapsed, they were confined to the temple, no torch, no food, no energy and no hope. As they waited for the moment to arrive they feared being turned into stone.

Chapter 2

As they waited, chills shivered down their spines. The slightest movement racked their nerves to pieces. 'We're as good as dead,' one of the explorers exclaimed!

'Stop your whining David!' shouted Markus, the leader of the expedition.

'It's all right for you, you didn't get sprayed by the elephant on the way here!' replied David. Then suddenly David yelled out in pain, 'Argh, something has got me!'

'What is it? What's happened? Ouch, what the …'

The explorers were bitten by a stray snake; there was no hope, unless they could find the vital antidote to prevent them turning into lifeless statues.

To be continued …

Robert Trippit (14)
The International School of Paphos, Cyprus

Inspired By A Dream

Solemnly on the forsaken beach, I observed the sky in the hour of darkness - the once comforting velvet blanket was now a cloak of doom that I simultaneously feared and was captivated by. The precious grains of sand slipped between my fingers, creating a connection between myself and nature; a bond which would shortly be corrupted forever.

The surrounding planets reflected an abnormal light across the serenity of the naïve ocean's edge. Nobody had predicted that they would break from their orbit like this - the scientists were cruelly deceived, rendering their years of research futile. Now they were heading agonisingly slowly towards Earth - the inevitable impact would be the moment when we would take our last breath, speak our final word and unwillingly torment our eyes with one disturbing, concluding image.

The intensity of my internal anger could only be expressed when glaring in mysterious contempt at the looming planets. They were strangely alluring, as their round forms dominated the void above. Their mere presence created a paranormal atmosphere - I observed the array of vivid colours swirling around on their surfaces, like an artist's palette after completing a masterpiece.

We had all anticipated engulfing flames that would entwine us in a macabre dance, or plummeting waves that would sweep away our very existence. Deep in my imagination, I had never foreseen an apocalypse like this. But that which was killing us was the psychological anguish of waiting … waiting for a resolution that would never come. Waiting for the imminent collision …

Megan Rex (17)
The International School of Paphos, Cyprus

Found In A Cave

Just the other day a young woman was walking to work, when there was a diversion so she went through the hills past an abandoned cave.

She was walking past when she heard a mumble and noises so she cautiously walked in trying not to get hurt.

'I walked in and saw a bright light at the end', said the woman. The woman said as she reached the end of the cave she saw a man huddled up against the wall in a blanket. She walked over and asked why he was there.

'I was worried, I was walking at night and got lost', he said. Later on that day the man admitted he was there for 2 weeks and wasn't eating or drinking. The man was sent to hospital but later recovered.

Katherine Courtney (13)
The International School of Paphos, Cyprus

Dangerous Monkey!

A monkey has escaped from a zoo in Chester. It escaped two days ago and has injured four people by kicking them in the back of the head. We think it is infected with a deadly diseases. It has gone crazy because of the rage it has been in.

If this monkey either scratches you or bites you, you could be in some danger. Please when you go out of your homes in Chester wear a hat because it may protect you a bit or if you can, wear a builder's helmet.

If you have a shotgun please take it with you for safety. Monkeys get scared when you hold something up to them.

Liam Park (13)
The International School of Paphos, Cyprus

Victoria Beckham Is Murdered

Footballer's wife and pop princess Victoria Beckham was found last night, stabbed in her jacuzzi, by her friend and maid, Laura Davies. She quotes, 'Me and Vic were supposed to be going clubbing and when I went to get her I saw her lying there in a pool of blood'.

Husband, David, is the prime suspect of the murder at the moment. This is because we are to believe that Victoria and David had an argument before Victoria stormed off to her jacuzzi for the last time …

Police have searched the Beckham house and found nothing, they are still looking for other clues to link other people to the murder.

David Beckham and Victoria's mum and dad, held a press conference earlier today begging for the murderer or anyone who knows anything about it to come forward to the police.

So far there has been no response, but it is early days yet.

Emma Moir (13)
The International School of Paphos, Cyprus

Global Warming

In the north of Cyprus in a fishing village, the houses are made of stone and mud. The roofs are made of palm trees, the floor is rags with mud. The people over there are very poor, but they do not know what global warming is doing to them.

The poor people have not seen what's happening to their houses and boats. The water has risen, soon their houses will be underwater.

As chief reporter for the Cyprus Daily, I am going to see for myself. The sea has risen, every day now I can see the sea rising a few centimetres. In the next two days I could see the water outside their front door. I can't imagine what they will do when their houses flood. They might be able to stay in their boats and live by eating fresh fish, but I think it's too cold to stay in their boats at night. I feel very sorry for these people, what will they do in the future?

Nicholas Nikolaou (13)
The International School of Paphos, Cyprus

A Day In The Life Of …

('While she was sleeping she dreamed that she could fly and later when she woke up her soul was in the sky!' Karen Shapiro)

The flight! You float in the pure sky and spring zephyr blows on you. You feel like a member of the passing by sky. Only birds may share these celestial feelings with you.

You fly but the breathing wind directs you. It swiftly raises you up to the zenith, where you feel all the beauty and nature in the universe. But it does not last long. The gusts are over you. They smoothly bring you down, onto the streets and now you rub against the rough asphalt. You are almost walking but you are not the only one. There are thousands like you, who try to battle for life. Some understand you and give the way, but others, having no aim they play back on you for all the torments they have had on the path of life.

You end up being crunched up and dishevelled, but happy for visiting the streets of your natal home. But can we call it a home? You have no home and no one knows where it is.

You have been ten times around the world. You were exported to all lands along and across. Then why did you choose this specific one? We may only make assumptions. Maybe you have been made here by machinery or the adventure was thrilling. I guess it is none of the above.

The reason for it being a home is that this town was the starting point of your long-lasting adventure. When the child lets you go, screaming, 'Go, *plastic bag*, go, with the wind's flow! and voyage around the world as I always dreamed of.'

Natasha Krikun (15)
The International School of Paphos, Cyprus

A Day In The Life Of A Depressed Teacher

From the second Mrs Elf awoke, her three kids were yelling at her for feeding. She made them all toast, then went to fetch the newspaper from the front porch for her husband. She had a quick glance. It was full of lunatic stories of bent politicians, flying saucers and evil vampire ducks going on killing sprees for mass vengeance.

At 8am, she left for work, at Wartytoad's Evil Brat School, where she worked full time as the citizenship teacher. Mrs Elf was nice to all every single day, but to be honest, now she was bored. All she desired now was to bludgeon every student to death with a chair. She hated Year 9 the most, as she felt they were a bunch of crack addicts with hippy parents, who were the spawn of Satan.

She entered the staffroom, where instantly, she was ridiculed.

'Oi, Elf, you lardy bag, teach better,' some shouted and, 'You suck!' and so on and so forth. Also, someone had taught the staff parrot to say, 'Elf is fat,' which it happily repeated all day.

Elf had become evil overnight. One child tried to misbehave, and she threw her board rubber at him. Another called her fat. She hung him off the fan by his pants and let him fly around the room.

Elf found life much more harmonious being evil. That was, of course, until someone dropped a piano on her.

Sam Griffiths (14)
The International School of Paphos, Cyprus

A Day In The Life Of A Janitor

'Stuck up cow!' muttered Billy. 'Doesn't even have the courtesy to say goodnight every once in a while!'

The door slammed and the slender-shaped headmistress stumbled out into the car park teetering on her party heels.

Billy turned and started off down the hallway dragging his mops 'n' bucket behind him. 'I need a new job!' exclaimed Billy. 'I'm sick 'n' tired of cleanin' the same pigsty, day in, day out, it's so boring!'

Full-handed, Billy kicked open the door to the janitor's closet, and dumped his stuff in the corner and sat down on an upturned bin reading his list of things to clean. 'Toilets, brilliant, it's always toilets, same old wee on the wall and bits of junk floating around in the over-flowing cubicles and they wonder why I'm here all day! Oh well, let's get it over and done with.' Billy pushed open the door and a foul smell swept through the corridor like a thick layer of fog. Billy pulled out the plunger and waded through the knee-deep swamp of sewage to the row of sinks which lay just at the other side of the room. Billy started to plunge and unblock the sinks while guiding currents of floating objects to the side.

Five hours later: Billy had finally got the school clean, the sinks were finally unblocked and now shining in the light of the overhead strip lights, the classrooms were all in order and blackboards were actually black.

'I think I'm going home now,' sighed Billy.

The door slammed and the school was empty!

Joshua Dixon (13)
The International School of Paphos, Cyprus

Alien Sighted!

An alien has been sighted in a swimming pool outside Michael Jackson's house. Some people say it was a child dressed up in an alien costume, but some say it was a real alien. What do you think? To see this clip which was caught on camera, please see our website on www.aliensightedinswimmingpool.com.

The alien was sighted around midnight. If you thought that the alien in the pool was weird then read on. The alien wasn't just relaxing in the pool, but it was drinking a beer, which the alien had stolen from the mini fridge in Michael Jackson's room. This story ends with the question, 'What was the alien doing in Michael Jackson's room anyway, when there were beers in the fridge in his kitchen?'

To find out the answer to the question please go on our website on www.answermyquestion. com.

Jack Baker (13)
The International School of Paphos, Cyprus

The Legend Of His Highness, Sir Tiziano, Emperor Of The Northern Ducks

For the ducks it was the time when food was rare, for the king it was money and diamonds, but for the knight, it was a mission to complete. It all started 70 years ago, when the seas were black from pollution from the king, and the houses didn't exist. Only one palace was in the city, it was the royal palace of the King of the Royal Ducks. He ruled with cruelty, his only love was for money and diamonds.

Twenty miles from the city there was a mine, a deep mine of diamonds. Dackard (Kingdom of the Northern Ducks) was the only kingdom which had a mine of diamonds so the King of the Southern Ducks was jealous and tried more than once to blow up the giant mine, but the King of the North did not care about all the ducks that died. The death rate in the mine was at least 100 ducks per month. All the ducks worked there because it was the only place they could earn money. The workers needed to bring the heavy diamonds on their back and walked for 20 miles to the city.

In secret, a group of workers that became stronger and stronger, decided to rebel against the king and kill him. So, one day, when the sky was black and it rained so much that the city was flooded, the ducks attacked the royal palace. Unfortunately the soldiers were ready for it and shot arrows at the ducks and many died.

Suddenly the rain stopped and a hole formed in the black clouds. A bright light passed through the holes and brought a bright light that went directly on an army, then he ran down and attacked the royal palace. After only 15 minutes of fighting in the palace, the flag of Dackard raised on the balcony and a soldier raised his masculine voice and announced, 'Your new king or better emperor is, His Highness, Sir Tiziano Emperor of the Northern Ducks!'

Sir Tiziano changed Dackard from white to black! The first thing he did was to build hundreds of palaces like the royal palace and make a bigger one for himself. He gave money to all the ducks and exploded the diamond mine and broke the border of war between Dackard and Nackard (Kingdom of the Southern Ducks) and wrote a document of peace to all the kingdoms around Dackard. The seas became blue and the clouds were not black any more.

Tiziano Bernard (12)
The International School of Trieste, Italy

The Mystery Of The Lake

This happened to Susan's grandmother. Susan is my best friend. Her grandmother was called Margaret. One day she was going to the lake to have a bath even though there was a scary legend about that mystic place, but she didn't mind. Margaret hurried so as not to feel fear and so that nobody would stop her.

She entered the lake and nothing happened. However, five minutes later, Margaret felt something strange, she was mystified. Suddenly, a dragon appeared from the other side of the lake and she screamed, 'Help me, help me! A dragon!'

A boy came through the wood although it was late! Margaret was never seen again.

They say that when you see the lake in the moonlight, people can see bubbles rising from the lake, like a dragon dancing with a woman …

Marina Franceschini (12)
Villa Devoto School, Buenos Aires

A Historical Meeting

Once upon a time in 1920 there was a scary rumour that spread all over New York. However, nobody knew the truth …

After the First World War, the vampires of Transylvania had a historical meeting. The leaders were at the central table discussing how to solve their problem. The oldest vampire started to talk, 'We all know that we have arranged this meeting in order to decide what we are going to do in the future. The population in Europe is decreasing and there aren't many young people with 'sweet blood' for all of us. If we don't take a decision quickly, we will soon have to suck the sour blood of cows again.'

Another one replied, 'Yes, it's true, I have heard that in America there are a lot of people with 'sweet blood'.'

Vampires in general are very allergic and they cannot suck just any kind of blood. So, they decided on moving to New York because there were many homeless in the streets and their task would be easier. Although, Dracula preferred Hollywood because he wanted to be a film star, he finally agreed with them.

Now they live in deserted subways and in underground sewers. Dracula also achieved his dream and his films became popular. As people never believed in fiction, this was part of his sinister plan to cover up the strange homicides in the subway. If you are young, be careful of taking the subway after midnight!

Heli García Álvarez (11)
Villa Devoto School, Buenos Aires

The Mysterious Man

Albert, the cousin of the friend of the brother of my best friend, told me that once he had gone to visit his aunt who had just lost her husband. After they had arrived at the house, Croatia, his aunt, opened the door and they entered. The house was really a cottage. It was old and big, although it was clean.

Croatia went to the supermarket in the town in order to buy food and soda water, and Albert's parents went with her. Albert and his little sister Mary were watching TV in Croatia's bedroom when suddenly a man appeared and offered them a glass of milk. They thought he was a servant so they accepted. The man brought the milk and they drank it all. He stayed all day with them, talking and laughing. In spite of being a servant he was very funny and jovial. Later, they heard someone knocking on the door; it was Croatia and his parents. The man went downstairs. Ten minutes later, his parents and Croatia turned up and they started talking. When Albert and Mary described the servant Croatia started crying, 'That was my husband!' she shouted.

Albert and Mary have never talked with strangers again. And there is a legend that says that if you ever happen to visit an aunt you haven't seen for years, watch out! There might be a friendly ghost at her place!

Martina Sáenz (12)
Villa Devoto School, Buenos Aires

An Angel Shot Down In The City

There was a couple who went to church every weekend. They were special in the town because they had never sinned. Their daughter, Milagros, was a beautiful smiling baby. Everyone was amazed because very young babies can't smile, but Milagros did.

As Milagros grew up her parents noticed that she didn't talk. That there was nothing wrong with her, as she was a very healthy child, but in her short life she had never said a single word.

On Milagros' fifteenth birthday she went to church, as she did every weekend. But while she was praying, a gang of thieves, who were being chased, rushed in forcing the policemen to go in behind them. It all happened so fast. There was a shot and Milagros came down on the floor, unconscious. The bullet had gone through her arm straight into her heart. Before she died, she muttered, 'I'm going home now.' And those were the only words that were ever heard from her.

Many years went by and this story had been forgotten in Luján until on Milagros' one hundredth death anniversary every angel in that Church lost its right wing in Milagros' honour.

I believe that Milagros' soul lives in every angel's body in that church and she is always there, protecting the children.

Andrea Liñán (12)
Villa Devoto School, Buenos Aires

The Mystifying Policeman

These two robberies happened to different people on the neighbourhood of 'Villa Devoto'.

The first one happened to the best friend of my grandmother's. It was the typical Sunday in which all the old ladies of Villa Devoto went to the supermarket. While they were there, one strange man broke into the supermarket and threatened everyone who was there to give him all their money. Frightened, everyone started shouting and the thief caught my grandmother's best friend as a hostage! She was really afraid! Despite kicking the thief and hitting him, he didn't let her go. Suddenly, in spite of the fact that no one had called him, a policeman appeared. Rapidly, he caught the thief and took him away. Sally (my grandmother's best friend) went to the police station so that she could make a statement and to thank the policeman, but no one at the police station had heard of that policeman, that was tall, thin and with blue eyes. Nobody had ever seen him. They only said that they had found a man tied over the bars of the police station with a notice which said, 'Put him in jail, he tried to rob a supermarket'. Everyone was mystified.

The second robbery happened to my grandmother, who was walking down a street, when a man took her wallet, where she had the money that she had recently taken from the bank. Suddenly, the same policeman appeared again!

Many people tried to catch the thief. However, they couldn't while the policeman could. He took him away and he tied him to the bars of the police station once more. He disappeared again.

A lot of incidents similar to these ones happened until the day that no one else tried to rob in Villa Devoto. As a result the policeman never appeared again, but the legend of the 'Mystifying Policeman' was still in the memory of all the people in Villa Devoto during the times of my grandparents.

Maria Lara Boz (12)
Villa Devoto School, Buenos Aires

The Beheaded Man

This happened to a group of kids that were in a park some years ago.

It was a very dark and gloomy night in the park. Arnold, Stinky and Gerald decided to go for a walk around the park because none of them were able to sleep.

Although they couldn't see so well they heard a dog barking and the sound of horses. Suddenly, Gerald saw a lovely grey dog and said, 'Oh what a lovely dog!' He grabbed him and asked, 'Who are you?'

Suddenly, he saw a kind of tag which said 'Pookie'. That was the dog's name.

Arnold laughed, 'Ha, ha! He is named like the little dog of the legend of the beheaded man.'

At that same moment they saw a man driving a carriage with two horses and they realised the driver was than man without a head.

They ran the fastest that they could and, although Stinky didn't know what to do, he also hurried in case something happened.

When the boys hid behind a tree somewhere there Stinky said, 'Why are we running boys?'

Arnold answered, 'Oh Stinky! Don't you know the legend about the man without a head?'

'No,' Stinky answered.

'I will tell you Stinky,' said Gerald. 'Once upon a time during a very cold night, a man drove carriages, picked up an old woman with a little lovely dog. The woman seemed to be in a hurry and shouted at the man, 'Faster, faster man! Hurry up please'. The man whipped the horses to go faster. When suddenly, his scarf rolled on and his head was cut off … However, the man was in such a hurry that he kept driving without his head … And the legend says that, every night at the same time, the same man appears in that park …'

Bárbara Testa (12)
Villa Devoto School, Buenos Aires